CHRISTIAN NAMES

Please return

JR Hoinby

Christian Names
for
Boys and Girls

Selected, compiled
and edited by
Tony Castle

Hodder & Stoughton
LONDON SYDNEY AUCKLAND

British Library Cataloguing in Publication Data
A record for this book is available from the British Library

ISBN 0 340 64223 8

Printed and bound in Great Britain by
Cox & Wyman Ltd, Reading, Berks

Hodder and Stoughton Ltd
A Division of Hodder Headline PLC
338 Euston Road
London NW1 3BH

Dedicated to 11A
who endured me as their Form Tutor
for five years

INTRODUCTION

Since the 1960s there has been a virtual explosion of new forenames augmenting the stock of long-established traditional ones. The multi-ethnic and multi-cultural nature of modern Britain has also swelled the pool of names to choose from and led to the demise of referring to a person's first name as his or her 'Christian' name. For well over a millenium, in Christian Europe, names were bestowed at Baptism and were referred to as 'baptismal' or 'Christian' names.

I recently heard the story of a vicar who refused to christen a child because the parents wanted to call him 'Pagan'; which would be a problem since Baptism is intended to take us from the heathen state into the family of God.

For every serious and committed Christian, Baptism is the most important event in their lives and, until recent times, this was marked and kept in memory by the bestowal of a name taken from the Bible or one of the eminent members of the family of God, that we call 'the Church'.

The seventeenth-century Puritans, who would have no truck with the Christian heroes of the past, whom we know as 'saints', searched the Bible for new biblical names. The tradition of keeping your 'name day', that is the special day of the saint you were named after was killed off, and the idea of celebrating 'birth days' instead was introduced. Even today in Christian countries, like Poland, 'name days' are kept and birthdays receive little attention.

In this book I have re-introduced 'name days'. I have given, after each name, where it is applicable, the 'special day' (shown as S.D.) for the biblical character or saint. Where it is known this is usually the day on which they were 'born into heaven' or died; failing that it is the traditional date given them on the Christian calendar. While I do not expect a nation-wide revival of an ancient practice, there may be parents who, having chosen a traditional Christian name, want their child to know and celebrate their name day.

Another tradition is to hand on a 'family' name, which may or may not be, strictly speaking, a 'Christian name'. My own two forenames illustrate both practices. The first entails a story. When my mother was expecting her first child (the writer), my father lost his job as a butcher because he dared to ask for a rise in salary, as my mother was just about to leave her secretarial post to have the baby. (No maternity leave in those days.) Suddenly both were unemployed during a period of wide-spread unemployment, just before the Second World War. There appeared to be no jobs about, but my mother, being a devout Roman Catholic, started praying, asking her favourite saint, St Anthony of Padua, to intercede for them. She promised that if her prayers were answered she would name her baby after him. On the fourth day, of the nine-day Novena of prayer, a stranger stopped my father in the street and asked him if he was looking for employment. He took the job and remained with the same company for the rest of his working life: and I became 'Anthony'.

My second forename is the family name, 'Percy' borne by my father and his father before him. However, my son's second name is Anthony; he has not inherited a name that I have never liked.

Choosing a name for a child is one of the most important post-birth decisions of parents. The bestowal of a personal name, for life, is a serious responsibility requiring careful thought and consideration. The name a child is known by can effect that child's self-perception and the perception of others. It can also reveal something of the child's culture and faith. For example a girl named 'Bernadette' is more likely (although not necessarily) to be from a practising Christian family than a child called 'Sandy'.

As a popular practical guide for parents I have kept the entries short and simple; answering the immediate questions: What does the name mean? Where does it come from? What are its Christian roots or how does it come to be a Christian name?

I was interested in compiling, what I hope will be, a useful and informative guide because I believe that it would be a tragic loss, with so many other ancient practices disappearing, if our traditional Christian names were squeezed out of existence by 'Waynes' and 'Kylies'. May 'Elizabeth' and 'Mary', 'Peter', 'James' and 'John' be as popular in a century's time as they have been for the last nineteen centuries.

Tony Castle, Harvest, 1995

BOYS' NAMES

A

Aaron   The name is probably Egyptian and its meaning is unknown. It was bestowed upon the elder brother of Moses while the Hebrews were captive in Egypt; he became the first High Priest of Israel (Exod. 6:13). There was also a sixth-century Celtic saint of this name. He lived as a hermit in Brittany; one of his disciples was St Malo. The name has been in regular use in the Jewish community for centuries. It was adopted by Nonconformist Christians in the seventeenth century.

S.D. 22nd June

Abel   The meaning of this name, probably derived from the Hebrew, is obscure, it may be derived from '*ablu*' meaning 'son'. One of the first names found in the Bible, he was the second son of Adam and Eve, murdered by his brother Cain (Gen. 4:1–16). It was traditionally used in the Christian litany for the dying. Popular among the seventeenth-century Puritans it is not much used in the twentieth century.

S.D. 2nd January

Abner   From the Hebrew, meaning 'father of light'. It is found in the Bible (1 Sam. 20:25) as the cousin of King Saul and commander of his army. While never popular in England, from the time of the Puritans it has been steadily used in the USA.

Abraham   From the Hebrew (in its original form of 'Abram' meaning 'high father') it was changed to Abraham (see Gen. 12:1ff) meaning 'father of multitudes'. He was the Patriarch, founder of the Jewish faith and progenitor of the Hebrew nation. Seven Christian saints, all obscure hermits or monks of the fourth–seventh centuries, bore the name. Always popular in Jewish usage; it only found general use in England among the Puritans of the seventeenth century. It is popular nowadays in many Christian parts of Africa.

S.D. 9th October

Achilles Although Greek, the meaning is obscure; the name of this Homeric hero was rarely used in Christian Europe, although there is one fourth-century saint (a). One of the Ugandan martyrs executed for the Christian faith in 1886 was named Achilleus (b).

(a) S.D. 15th May (b) S.D. 3rd June

Adam Of uncertain origin it probably comes from the Hebrew word *'adama'* meaning 'earth'; and as such was the name given to the first man, who came from the earth (see Gen. 2:4–25). There are two thirteenth-century saints, both monks, of the name. At that period it was one of the most common names in England; it lost popularity for several hundred years but it has returned to common use in modern times.

S.D. 24th December

Adlai The name of a very minor biblical character (1 Chr. 27:29) popularised by seventeenth-century Puritans. Taken to North America by the early settlers, where it is still common.

Adrian This is the English form of the Latin 'Hadrianus' (man from Hadria, a town of Northern Italy). The name of a Roman Emperor, and several popes. The only English pope, Nicholas Breakspear (d. 1159), took the name Adrian IV. There have been eight saints of this name. The most famous was a Benedictine monk and headmaster of St Augustine's school, Canterbury; he died in 710.

S.D. 9th January

Aidan The English version of the Gaelic 'Aedan', or the old English 'AEthan' derived from '*aed*' meaning 'fire'. The name of three early Irish saints, the most important being the seventh-century monk of Iona who, using Lindisfarne, of which he was bishop, converted Northumberland. The name was revived in nineteenth-century England.

S.D. 31st August

Alan A Celtic name, the origins and meaning of which are uncertain. There was a popular early Welsh saint of this name (fifth century). The name became established in England as a result of the Norman Conquest. The form 'Alain' was more common then, also 'Alein' and 'Allen'.

S.D. 26th October

Alban The name of the first British martyr (fourth-century) who died at Verulam, now known as St Albans. In art he is shown with a sword and a tall cross. Never very popular, it was revived in the nineteenth century. Derived from it is 'Albany' and 'Albion'.

S.D. 20th June

Alberic Comes from the Old German 'Albirich'. There were four saints of the Benedictine Order of this name; the most well-known, of the twelfth century, was one of the three founders of the Cistercian Order.

S.D. 26th January

Albert Comes from the French, but is Germanic in origin; it was brought to England by the Normans. It was popular in the nineteenth century to honour Queen Victoria's husband, Prince Albert. It means noble and illustrious. Very popular among the saints, there are twenty-one with this name; the most famous was Albert the Great (1200–80), a brilliant theologian and teacher of Thomas Aquinas. He was declared a Doctor of the Church (RC) in 1931.

S.D. 15th November

Alexander   A popular name in the post-classical period, this derives from the fame of Alexander the Great. Several New Testament characters and a host of early Christian martyrs bore the name. The most recent saint is Alexander Briant, a Jesuit priest, executed at Tyburn in 1581. It means 'helper and protector of man'.

S.D. 1st December

Alexis   From 'Alexius' (Latin version of the Greek 'Alexios') derived from '*alexein*' meaning 'to defend'. St Alexius lived in the fifth century, his life is surrounded by legend; venerated in the Orthodox Church, the name is common in Russia. In the West it has also been given to girls.

S.D. 17th July

Alfred   Comes from the Old English, AElfaed, meaning 'wise counsel of the elf'. Alfred the Great (849–99) was King of Wessex, patron of learning, defender of the Church against the Danes and venerated in Christian England as a saint. He was regarded as the pattern of Christian kingship. The name, in various forms, spread widely throughout Europe; popular in nineteenth-century England, its use has waned this century.

S.D. 26th October

Aloysius (also **Ludovicus**)   The Latin form of the French name 'Louis'. Two saints have borne this name; the most famous, especially in Roman Catholic circles, is the sixteenth-century Aloysius Gonzaga, a member of the Society of Jesus, who died from nursing plague victims, when only twenty-two. Canonized in 1726, he was declared patron of Catholic Youth in the twentieth century.

S.D. 21st June

Alphonsus   Originally an Old German name, meaning 'noble and ready', it was taken to Spain, where as 'Alphonso', 'Alfonso' or 'Alonso' it became a favourite name. Not surprisingly it was the name of nine Spanish saints. However, the most famous saint of this name was from Naples. Alphonsus Ligouri, 1696–1787, was a theologian, Bishop, and founder of the Redemptorist Congregation of Priests.

S.D. 1st August

Amasa   Of Hebrew origin, meaning 'burden bearer'. A captain of Absalom's army (2 Sam. 19:13) who succeeded Joab as David's commander-in-chief.

Ambrose   This is the English form of the Latin 'Ambrosius' meaning 'immortal'. Twelve saints, sprinkled through history, bore this name; the most illustrious was Ambrose, the fourth-century Bishop of Milan. Famous for being one of the greatest bishops of Christian history. The name has been more popular in Ireland than in England.

S.D. 7th December

Amos   A Hebrew name, probably from the verb '*amos*', to carry. This has been interpreted by some to mean, 'borne by God'. The name of one of the minor Old

Testament prophets; the book of the Bible, named after him, carries references to his life as a shepherd and dresser of sycamore trees. Although not much used in modern England it was popular among the Puritans and retains some popularity in the USA.

S.D. 31st March

Andreas The original Greek form of 'Andrew', sometimes used as variant.

Andrew A popular European name that appears in several variants; it comes from the Greek for 'manly'. According to John's Gospel he was the first disciple to be called by Jesus, to whom he introduced his brother Simon Peter. The Apostle Andrew was a very popular saint in medieval Europe; he was adopted as patron saint of Russia, Greece and Scotland. His emblem in art is the traditional cross of his martyr-dom (supposedly crucified at Patras, Achaia). Twenty-one other Christian saints bear this name.

S.D. 30th November

Anselm An Old German name meaning 'divine helmet'. It was chiefly used by the Lombards and it was St Anselm (1033–1109), a Lombard, who brought the name first to England when he was appointed Arch-bishop of Canterbury. A brilliant scholar, he had a stormy career opposing the demands of the English monarch. Never really popular in England, it enjoyed a revival of interest in the nineteenth century.

S.D. 21st April

Antony A well-established European name (meaning 'of ines-timable worth') that comes from the Greek, 'Anthon-ios', or Latin, 'Antonius'; hence there are two versions of the name, one with, and one without, the 'h'. The early popularity of the name is due to the St Antony (251–356) the first Christian hermit, then monk, who lived in Eygpt (a). The later popularity is due to the fame of Anthony of Padua, a gifted Franciscan preacher, who died at Padua (b). He is popularly invoked to help find lost objects; represented in art carrying the child Jesus. There are hosts of other lesser-known saints of the same name.

(a) S.D. 17th January (b) S.D. 13th June

Archibald Originates from the Old German 'Ercanbald' and means 'noble and truly bold'. There was no biblical character or saint of this name, but it entered Christian usage because the Anglo-Saxon, pre-Conquest, St Eorkonweald (d. 693) was sometimes referred to as St Archibald. It was used in the North of England and was particularly popular in Scotland.

Arnold Comes from the Old German 'Arenvald', meaning 'strong as an eagle'. The Normans brought the name to England as 'Arnaud'. The original saint (there are two others) was a Greek (d. 800) who was famous for his charity to the poor.

S.D. 8th July

Asa A biblical name (see 1 Kgs 15:9ff) borne by a King of Judah, son of Abijah, who reigned for forty years. Of Hebrew origin, it means 'doctor' or 'healer'. Apart from Jewish usage it was first used in Christian circles in the seventeenth century by the Puritans; only rarely in the twentieth century.

Augustine (also **Austin**) A popular name throughout Europe, particularly in England, during the Middle Ages, when the 'Austin' form was in common use. It comes from the Latin 'Augustus' meaning 'venerable'. There are nine saints of this name, the most influential were Augustine of Hippo (fourth century), one of the greatest thinkers of the Western Church (a) and the first Archbishop of Canterbury (sixth century) who brought Christianity to Kent (b).

(a) S.D. 28th August (b) S.D. 27th May

B

Baldwin Germanic in origin the name, meaning 'bold friend', became popular in Flanders and was introduced into England by the Normans. There was a lesser-known Benedictine saint of the twelfth century, but no other particular Christian usage is evident. Though less common in modern times it has not completely disappeared.

S.D. 15th July

Baptist Originating from the Latin *'baptista'* (one who baptises) the name is usually used with 'John'. Although uncommon in either form in England, it is much used in Roman Catholic countries and among some evangelical sects in the USA.

Barnabas Hebrew in origin, the name means 'son of consolation'. A companion of St Paul, Barnabas was never an Apostle but because of the many references to him in the New Testament he has always been honoured as one. Tradition has it that he died a martyr in Cyprus. In art he is always depicted as standing near a pile of stones and holding a book. The name has been used in England since about 1200; however, the variants 'Barnaby', 'Barnabe' or 'Barney' have been more commonly used.

S.D. 11th June

Barnard   *(See Bernard.)*

Bartholomew   The name of one of the twelve Apostles, it is Hebrew in origin, meaning 'son of Talmai' or 'son of the furrows'. In the New Testament he is also known as 'Nathaniel'. The name was very common in England and throughout Europe from the twelfth century onwards, which is attested by there being thirteen other saints of this name.

S.D. 24th August

Baruch   A biblical name of Hebrew origins meaning 'blessed'. The name of the prophet Jeremiah's secretary and companion (Jer. 32:12) also of two lesser-known characters (see Neh. 3:20 and Neh. 10:6). Used as a Christian name from the sixteenth century, especially in the Midlands; not common in the twentieth century.

Basil   From the Greek meaning 'kingly'. Popular throughout the Eastern Church due to the reverence given to St Basil the Great, (*c.* 330–79) Bishop of Caesarea and theologian. He is considered one of the three founding Fathers of the Eastern Church and one of the four great Doctors (teachers) of the Western Church. There were several other lesser-known saints of the same name. It was used in England from the end of the twelfth century; its use was revived, in the nineteenth century, in the High Church of the Church of England.

S.D. 2nd January

Benedict   Very popular throughout the Middle Ages (there are twenty-one saints of this name) it comes from the Latin 'Benedictus' meaning 'Blessed' or 'One blessed by God'. Its popularity springs from the saint (*c.*

480–550) who founded the famous Benedictine Order of monks and gave the Christian world a model of a monastic rule and life. He began as a hermit at Subiaco, central Italy, gathered many followers and moved to Monte Cassino, where he founded the great monastery. His life and work is considered one of the most powerful factors in the building up of civilisation in Christian Europe. He was declared patron of Europe in 1964.

S.D. 11th July

Benjamin   This name appears three times in the Bible (Gen. 35:18; 1 Chr. 7:10; Ezra 10:32) but it usually calls to mind the youngest son of Jacob. He was first named 'Benoni' meaning 'son of my sorrow' by his mother Rachel, who died shortly after his birth. However, his father renamed him 'Benjamin' meaning 'son of the south'. More usually a Jewish name, it was used as a Christian name in England after the Reformation; declined in use during the nineteenth century but returned to popularity in the late twentieth century (short form – Ben). There was one, rather obscure, saint of this name who died a martyr in 421.

S.D. 31st March

Bernard   Originates from the Old German 'Berinhard' meaning 'brave as a bear'. Used throughout the Continent (witness twelve European saints of this name) it became particularly popular due to the influence of St Bernard of Methon (d. 1081) who for forty years served travellers in the Alps, founding two hospices in the passes that bear his name (a). (The famous rescue-dog is named after him.) St Bernard of Clairvaux (1090–1153) influential founder of the Cistercian Order (he founded sixty-eight monasteries) (b);

great theologian, writer and adviser of popes, kings and councils. Use of the name declined at the Reformation but experienced a revival in nineteenth-century England. The diminutive 'Bernie' is used in the USA.

(a) S.D. 28th May (b) S.D. 20th August

Bertram Some claim this to be, in origin, an Anglo-Saxon name, others Old French or Germanic; its meaning is 'bright raven'. It was certainly used in England after the Norman Conquest; in several varied forms, 'Bertran', 'Bartram' or 'Bertrand'; with the diminutive, 'Bertie'. There are two obscure Christian saints of the seventh and eighth centuries who bore the name.

S.D. 24th January or 6th September

Blaise (or Blase) Probably comes from the Latin '*blaesus*', meaning 'stammerer'. It was a very popular name in medieval England because St Blaise, Bishop of Sebaste, martyred in 316, was patron saint of the influential woolworkers. Legend has it that he saved the life of a boy who was choking on a fish bone. In the Roman Catholic Church there is a traditional blessing of throats on his feast day.

S.D. 3rd February

Boniface From the Latin '*bonifacius*' meaning 'one who does good'. Not common nowadays it was, however, very popular in England from the thirteenth century to the Reformation. The original saint was a third-century Christian martyred at Tarsus; besides a series of popes, twelve later saints shared the name. The most important by far being the Anglo-Saxon Benedictine monk (680–754) who took

Christianity to Germany (called 'the Apostle of the Germans).

S.D. 5th June

Brendan A Gaelic name derived from '*breanainn*' meaning 'prince'. The modern Irish form (where it is frequently used) 'Breandan' and the English version are based on the Latin 'Brendanus'. There were two sixth-century saints, Brendan the Voyager (a) who is believed to be the first European to sail to North America, and Brendan of Birr (b). The first is one of the three most famous saints of Ireland and patron of sailors.

(a) S.D. 16th May (b) S.D. 29th November

Brice Of Celtic origin the name means 'quick', 'ambitious'. It was much in vogue in England and France during the Middle Ages due to St Brice, Bishop of Tours (444), a popular disciple of the great St Martin of Tours.

S.D. 13th November

Bruno From the German '*brun*' meaning 'brown'. The existence of five saints of this name in the tenth–eleventh centuries attest to its wide use throughout Europe in the Middle Ages. The most prominent being the son of the Emperor Henry the Fowler, who was Archbishop of Cologne (a). Another was Bruno of Chartreuse, the founder of the Carthusian Order who died in 1101 (b).

(a) S.D. 11th October (b) S.D. 6th October

C

Caleb   A biblical name from the Hebrew meaning 'bold' or 'impetuous'; it appears twice in the Bible. The son of Hezron (1 Chr. 2:18) and the better known son of Jephunneh (Num. 13:6) who spied out the Promised Land with Joshua. He alone, of the original Hebrew slaves to leave Egypt, enters the Promised Land with Joshua (Num. 26:65). The name was popular in Puritan times and taken by them to the USA, where it is still in use.

Calum   This originates from the Latin word '*columba*' meaning 'dove', via the Scottish Gaelic tradition. It was very popular in early Christian times because of the symbolism of the dove representing peace, gentleness and the Holy Spirit. The great St Columba was the most famous of the saints of Scotland. He founded many monasteries in Ireland and Scotland and is revered as the missionary of the North and the founder of the monastery of Iona.

S.D. 9th June

Calvin   Originates from the French surname of the Protestant theologian Jean Calvin (1509–64); used, mainly in the USA, by Christians of the Reformed Tradition. As a surname the name meant 'little bald one'.

Carl   Increasingly popular in the English-speaking world, it is a variant of 'Karl', the German version of Charles (*see Charles*).

Casimir   Of Slavic origin the name means 'proclaimer of peace'. St Casimir was a fifteenth-century Polish prince who resisted the evil political plans of his father. As patron of Poland and Lithuania the name is found mostly among Roman Catholics of Eastern European origins.

S.D. 4th March

Caspar   A Persian name meaning 'Master of the treasure'. It is one of the legendary names given to the Magi who journeyed from the East to visit the child Jesus. The Bible, however, (Matt. 2:1) does not record how many there were or their names. Several saints and holy persons, particularly of the seventeenth century were named after the legendary figure. Variants are Jasper (Dutch form) and Casper.

S.D. 6th January

Cathal (variants **Cathaldus** and **Cataldus**)   An Irish name for 'Charles' or 'Carl' derived from the old Celtic words for 'battle' and 'ruler'. It was borne by the seventeenth-century Irish saint who originated from Munster but became, eventually, Bishop of Taranto in Southern Italy.

S.D. 10th May

Chad   This is the modern spelling of the Anglo-Saxon 'Ceadda' which may mean 'warlike'. The seventeenth-century saint of this name, brother of St Cedd, was educated at Lindisfarne and became Archbishop of York, and then of Lichfield.

S.D. 2nd March

Charles   A popular European name with many variants, Carl, Carlos, Carol, Karol, Cary etc. It originates from the German word meaning 'free man'. Its popularity sprang at first from the Frankish leader, Charles the Great or Charlemagne, who in 800 became the Holy Roman Emperor. The Church confirmed popular devotion by allowing the Emperor the title 'Blessed'. There followed eight other saintly men, the most famous being Charles Borromeo (1538–84) the influential Counter-Reformation Bishop of Milan. The name was introduced into England by Mary Queen of Scots and so became established as a royal name.

S.D. 4th November

Christian   From the Latin 'Christianus' the name first given to the followers of Christ at Antioch (Acts 11:26) about year 60, previously called 'People of the Way'. The word 'Christ' is the Greek equivalent of the Hebrew word 'Messiah' meaning 'anointed'. Used as a given name in England, from time to time, since the twelfth century. The only saint was the twelfth-century Irish Bishop of Clogher.

S.D. 12th June

Christopher   Popular European name, it comes from the Greek meaning 'the Christ-bearer'. It was originally a word used by Christians and applied to themselves, meaning that they bore Christ by faith in their hearts. There was an obscure early Christian martyr who died at Lycia in Roman times. His name has attracted many legends, the most beautiful is the commonly known story that he carried an unknown child across a ford; the child was Christ. The story led to the usual representation of the saint in art and popular devotion. The patron of travellers, in Roman Catholic countries he is regarded particularly as the patron of motorists. One of the most popular of the medieval saints his name is used widely throughout Europe.

S.D. 25th July

Ciaran An Irish Gaelic name that has been translated in England as 'Kieran', meaning 'small and dark-skinned'. Two sixth-century Irish saints, who helped in the Christianisation of Ireland, bore the name.

S.D. 5th March or 9th September

Cillian Recognised in English as 'Kilian' (or 'Killian') this Gaelic name meaning 'little warlike one', comes from three seventh-century Irish saints.

S.D. 8th or 29th July

Claude The French version of the original Latin, 'Claudius'; it is derived from '*claudus*' which means 'lame'. There were seven early Christian martyrs (third and fourth centuries) of this name but its popularity in France is due to St Claude of Besancon, a seventh century abbot and bishop.

S.D. 6th June

Claus German version of 'Nicholas' (*see Nicholas*).

Clem Short form of Clement (*see Clement*).

Clement Derived from the Latin '*clemens*' meaning 'merciful'; this was a very popular Christian name, borne throughout Church history by thirteen very different saints. St Clement I was the third successor of St Peter in the See of Rome; there were thirteen further popes of the same name, the last in the eighteenth century.

S.D. (St Clement of Alexandria) 4th December

Colin This comes from the French diminutive of 'Col', short for 'Nicholas'. It means 'strong and virile'. The name is found in England from the thirteenth century and gave rise to the surnames 'Collins' and 'Collinson' (a). The Scottish 'Colin' comes from a different root: it is believed that it comes from the Gaelic 'Cailean', which relates to St Columba (b).

(a) S.D. St Nicholas 6th December (b) S.D. 9th June

Colum (or Colm)   The Irish form of 'Columba', from the Latin for 'dove'. St Columba (521–97) was the missionary who took the Christian faith to the Picts of Northern England and Scotland. He is more usually known as 'Columcille'.

S.D. 9th June

Conan   Derived from the Old Celtic meaning 'high and mighty'. There were several obscure Irish saints of this name, the better known being the seventeenth-century monk of Iona who became bishop in the Isle of Man.

S.D. 26th January

Conrad   The English version of the German name 'Konrad' meaning 'brave counsellor'. There were five saints of this name, the most prominent being Conrad of Constance, a tenth century bishop. Essentially a German name it has occasionally been used in England, particularly from the nineteenth-century.

S.D. 26th November

Cormac   An ancient Irish name, common in Irish myths and legends, of uncertain origin and meaning. Two Irish saints bore the name, the more famous being the tenth-century first Bishop of Cashel.

S.D. 14th September

Cornelius   Originating from an old Roman family name it probably means 'horn'. This was the name of the devout Roman centurion, stationed at Caesarea who was converted by Peter (Acts 10:1–40). Also the name of a third-century martyred pope and three other saints. Used throughout Europe it has been most popular in the Low Countries.

S.D. 16th September

Cosmo (or Cosmas)   This is the Italian version of the Greek name 'Kosmas' which means 'order'. Several saints bear this name, the most well-known being one of the twins, Cosmas and Damian. They were doctors who gave their services to the poor for nothing and died as martyrs under the Emperor Diocletian, *c.* 303. They were very popular throughout Europe during the Middle Ages and many beautiful legends of caring for the sick grew up around them. The name was brought to Britain in the eighteenth century and found occasional use in Scotland.

S.D. 26th September

Crispin (Crispian)   From the Latin 'Crispinus', a Roman name, probably meaning 'curly-headed'. Very popular in medieval times there are seven saints with the name. The first, and most popular, was the shoe-maker (hence St Crispin is the patron of shoemakers) who died a martyr's death at Soissons, France *c.* 285.

S.D. 25th October

Cuthbert   Although now out of fashion this was a common Old English name (meaning 'bright and famous') from before the Norman Conquest. Two bishop-saints bore the name; Cuthbert of Lindisfarne (d. 687) one of the most famous of English saints, whose tomb at Durham was a popular place of pilgrimage where many miracles were recorded (a). Cuthbert, Archbishop of Canterbury (d. 758) of whom little is known. Modern Roman Catholics recall St Cuthbert Mayne (1544–77) who was executed at Launceston for celebrating Mass when it was a crime under Elizabeth I (b).

(a) S.D. 4th September (b) S.D. 29th November

Cyprian From the Latin name 'Cyprianus' meaning 'native of Cyprus'. The great St Cyprian of Carthage (*c.* 200–58) was one of the first important Christian writers. He wrote several important books and was beheaded during the Diocletian persecution of Christians. Several other less-distinguished saints bear the same name.

S.D. 16th September

Cyril Probably from the Greek word '*kyrios*' meaning 'lord'. It was a popular name among the early Christians, attested by the twelve saints of the early centuries. In addition the famous theologians and teachers, Cyril of Jerusalem (a) (d. 386) and Cyril of Alexandria (b) (d. 444); there was also St Cyril, 'the Apostle of the Slavs' (c), who with his brother Methodius, took Christianity to the Slavonic regions of Eastern Europe. The name does not appear to have been used in England before the seventeenth century, but became popular in the nineteenth century.

(a) S.D. 18th March (b) S.D. 27th June (c) S.D. 14th February

D

Dafydd The Welsh form of David (*see David*).

Damian (Damien) Probably derived from the Greek word '*daman*' meaning 'to tame'; the name may also be taken from the Greek classical name, 'Damon'. There are several lesser-known saints, however, the best known is the brother of St Cosmas (*see Cosmos*). Modern Roman Catholics are more likely to associate the name with Father Damien (1840–89), the heroic missionary to the lepers on Molokai, a Pacific island. The name was in use in England from the thirteenth century.

S.D. 26th September

Dan This can be a shortening of 'Daniel' or a name in its own right. It is a Hebrew word meaning 'he judged' and was the name given to Jacob's son by Bilhah, Rachel's maid (Gen. 30:6).

Daniel A Hebrew word meaning 'the Lord is my judge'. There are two Daniels in the Bible; the first was the son of David and Abigail (1 Chr. 3:1); the second, Daniel the prophet, is the more important. His story is told in the Book of Daniel. The story of him in the lions' den was very popular in medieval miracle plays, so the name was commonly used. There are eight Christian saints bearing the name, none of great note. Used in England from before the Norman Conquest, it went out of vogue in the nineteenth century but it is once more back in fashion.

S.D. 21st July

David Originally this was a Hebrew lullaby word meaning 'darling' then 'friend' or 'beloved'. This was one of the titles of the great King David, beloved of God, shepherd-son of Jesse, who succeeded Saul as King of Judah and Israel (a). He is credited with many of the Psalms and is one of the types of Christ in the Old Testament. His story is told in 1 and 2 Samuel. One of the first bearers of the name in Britain was Dewi, or David, Archbishop of Menevia (d. 600);

patron saint of Wales (b). From his time the name has been a favourite one in Wales, although never very popular in England, until recent times. There are four other saints, the most recently canonised was David Lewis (1616–79) a Jesuit priest who was executed at Usk for celebrating Mass, when it was punishable by death.

(a) S.D. 29th December (b) S.D. 1st March

Declan The English form of the Irish 'Deaglan' of uncertain meaning. St Declan was the fifth-century disciple of St Colman who became bishop in the district of Ardmore, Ireland. The name has become popular in modern Ireland.

S.D. 24th July

Dennis (Denis) From the Latin 'Dionysius' which is from the Greek, and referred to a devotee of the Greek god, Dionysos. The name was very popular in the early centuries of Christianity; there being over twenty saints, mostly martyrs, of this name. Its popularity in Europe, particularly in France, derives from the third-century missionary to the Gauls, who was martyred near Paris in 272 and adopted as patron saint of France. Commonly found in England (there are forty-one churches dedicated to the saint) up to the seventeenth century, when it dropped out of vogue; it returned to popular usage at the beginning of the twentieth century.

S.D. 9th October

Dominic A truly European name, originating from the Latin 'dominicus' meaning 'belonging to the Lord', it is found in a variety of forms ('Dominique' French; 'Domingo' Spanish; 'Domenico' Italian; etc.). Originally the name may have been given to children born on a Sunday (*dies dominca*). It appears as a Christian name in the thirteenth century in honour of St Dominic (1170–1221) founder of the Order of Preachers (Dominicans) which exerted a powerful influence throughout Europe (a). However, there were four saints of this name prior to the thirteenth century and eleven after, the most famous of the latter being St Dominic Savio (1842–57), the youngest non-martyr saint in history (b).

Never common in England before the Reformation, after it was almost exclusively used by Roman Catholics. In recent years it has gained more general usage.

(a) S.D. 8th August (b) S.D. 8th March

Donald From the Gaelic 'Domhnall' meaning 'ruler of the world', this was originally a Scottish name associated with the MacDonald clan, the medieval Lords of the Isles. There was an eighth-century Scottish St Donald, who lived at Ogilivy in Forfarshire.

S.D. 15th July

Dunstan Meaning 'dark stone' from the Old English, this was the name of the great saintly Archbishop of Canterbury (909–88) who was much revered in the Middle Ages. The name went out of use after the Reformation but was revived in the nineteenth century.

S.D. 19th May

E

Eamon The Gaelic form of 'Edmund' (*see Edmund*).

Ebenezer From the Hebrew meaning 'stone of help'. The word appears in the Bible as the name of the stone raised by Samuel (1 Sam. 7:12) to commemorate the defeat of the Philistines. Introduced by seventeenth-century Puritans as a personal name, it is still used in the USA.

Eden Used for males and females, it would appear to have originated from the Hebrew word, from Genesis 2:8, the Garden of 'delight'. Mainly found in the USA.

Edgar An Old English name 'Eadgar' meaning 'wealthy spearman'. It was used in the royal house of Wessex and survived the Norman Conquest. St Edgar the Peaceful (d. 975) was the English king who had St Dunstan as his adviser. Not in use from thirteenth to nineteenth century, when revived by the Romantics.

S.D. 8th July

Edmond The French form of Edmund (*see Edmund*).

Edmund Meaning 'rich guardian' from the Old English 'Eadmund'. There were two English kings (in addition to the martyr-king) of this name and several noteworthy saints. King Edmund (849–69), King of the East Angles, killed for his faith by invading Danes in Suffolk (a). St Edmund Rich (1180–1242) scholar and Archbishop of Canterbury (b) and also three priests who were hung, drawn and quartered during the Elizabethan persecution of the Catholic Church; Edmund Arrowsmith, Edmund Campion and Edmund Gennings.

(a) S.D. 20th November (b) S.D. 20th November

Edward From the Old English 'Eadweard' meaning 'prosperous ruler'; it is one of the few names popular throughout Europe for hundreds of years that originated from England. The name of three Anglo-Saxon kings and eight kings since the Norman Conquest. It is the influence of the Anglo-Saxons that established it as a popular Christian name; Edward the Elder, son of Alfred the Great (d. 924); St Edward (the Martyr (d. 979) and the famous St Edward the Confessor (d. 1066), considered the model king; he also built Westminster Abbey. The popularity of the name in Elizabethan times is attested to by the fact that twelve of the Roman Catholic martyrs of the period were named Edward.

S.D. (Edward the Confessor) 13th October

Edwin   Meaning 'prosperous friend' from the Old English 'Eadwine'. Borne by the first Christian king of Northumbria, when he fell in battle against the pagan Mercians, he was venerated as a martyr. Out of use for centuries it was revived as a personal name in the nineteenth century.

S.D. 12th October

Eli   Hebrew name meaning 'height'; it was borne by the high priest who brought up the prophet Samuel (1 Sam. 1–4). It was adopted by the seventeenth-century Puritans and is occasionally found in the USA.

Elias   The Greek form of the Hebrew name 'Elijah' (*see Elijah*).

Elijah   Hebrew name from the Bible meaning 'Yahweh (Lord) is God'. The great prophet of the Old Testament whose eventful life can be found in 1 and 2 Kings. Because it was one of the most popular Old Testament names in the Middle Ages, the following names are derived from it; 'Ellis', 'Elie' (French), 'Elley', 'Elliot(t)' and 'Eliot'.

S.D. 20th July

Eliot (Elliott)   (*See Elijah.*)

Elvis   (*See Elwyn.*)

Elwyn (Elwin, Elvis)   Of Celtic origin the name means 'friend of the elves', but its origin is uncertain. There was an obscure Irish saint of the sixth century called St Elwyn or St Elvis.

S.D. 22nd February

Emanuel (or Emmanuel)   The New Testament Greek of the Hebrew word 'Immanuel' meaning 'God with us'; a Messianic title found in Isaiah 7:14 and applied to Christ by Matthew 1:23. It found popularity in Latin countries as 'Manuel' or 'Manoel', but not much used in the English-speaking world. Three little-known saints bore the name.

S.D. (various including) 31st July

Enoch   Hebrew name which possibly means 'dedicated' or 'skilled'. There were two biblical characters of this name: the son of Cain (Gen. 4:16) and the father of Methuselah (Gen. 5:18). There is an apocryphal book of the Bible attributed to him (see Jude v. 14). An obscure Scottish saint (d. 1007) bore the name.

S.D. 25th March

Ephraim   The name of the second son of Joseph; a Hebrew name probably meaning 'fruitful' (see Gen. 41:52). There was a St Ephraem the Syrian (d. 373) who wrote biblical commentaries. Still used in the Jewish community; since the eighteenth century it has occasional use in the USA.

S.D. 9th June

Erasmus   From the Greek for 'beloved' or 'desired'. St Erasmus (d. 303) was a bishop who was martyred under the Emperor Diocletian; very popular in the Middle Ages and accepted as patron of sailors. The name is better known from the Dutch Humanist scholar, Desiderius Erasmus (1465–1536). Not much used in modern times.

S.D. 2nd June

Eric   Scandinavian name from the Old Norse meaning 'powerful ruler'. There was a St Eric, King of Sweden (d. 1160) who attempted to establish a Christian kingdom and was murdered for his faith. Introduced into Britain by the Danes, the name dropped out of use and was reintroduced in mid-nineteenth century.

S.D. 18th May

Ethan   A Hebrew name, meaning 'steadfast and firm', borne by two little-known people in the Bible (e.g. 1 Kgs 4:31). Introduced into the USA by the Puritans, the name is still in occasional use.

Eugene   The Old French form of the Greek name 'Eugenios' meaning 'nobly born'. Very popular name in the early years of the Church; there are fourteen saints and four popes. Infrequently found in Britain, it is more popular in the USA, where it is sometimes shortened to 'Gene'.

S.D. 13th November

Eustace   Originating from the Greek meaning 'fruitful', the name was borne by eight Christian saints, the most recent being the Lincolnshire priest, St Eustace White, a Roman Catholic martyr of Elizabethan times.

S.D. 10th December

Ezekiel Hebrew name meaning 'may God strengthen' was the name of one of the three major prophets, who prophesied among the Israelites in captivity in Babylon. The name was adopted in seventeenth-century England and continues to be used in the USA.

S.D. 10th April

Ezra Hebrew name meaning 'the one who helps', belonged to the Old Testament scribe (fourth–fifth century) to whom is credited a book of the Bible. First used in England in the seventeenth century the name is still used in the USA and parts of Africa.

S.D. 13th July

F

Fabian The name of two early Christian saints, one a pope, comes from the Latin name 'Fabianus'; its meaning is not clear, but it could mean 'prosperous farmer'. Introduced by the Normans into England it has never been widely used.

S.D. 20th January

Felix From the Latin *'felix'* meaning 'happy' or 'fortunate', it appears in the New Testament (Acts 23–24) and was one of the most popular names among the early Christians. There are at least seventy-four saints in the Christian calendar, and four popes, most of whom are martyrs of the second–fourth centuries. It was popular in medieval England due to St Felix of Dunwich (d. 647) who preached Christianity to the East Angles; the town of Felixstowe was named after him.

S.D. 8th March

Ferdinand Although of Germanic origin meaning 'bold adventurer', it became very popular in Spain, where it was used by the kings of Castille. In the sixteenth century the Italian version 'Ferdinando' became popular in England. There are two Spanish saints of this name, one of whom was Ferdinand III, King of Castille (1198–1252).

S.D. 30th May

Fergus An Old Irish name meaning 'the best choice'. There was a St Fergus of Scotland (d. 721) an Irish bishop who worked in Perthshire, and it was the name of the grandfather of the great St Columba. Its main use is still found in Ireland and Scotland.

S.D. 27th November

Finbar The English form of the Gaelic, 'Fionnbarr', meaning 'white-head'. There are two Irish saints of this name, both of the sixth century. The better known was the first Bishop of Cork. The name is more often found in families of Irish descent.

S.D. 4th July

Finian (Finnian) Irish name derived from '*finnen*' meaning 'white' or 'fair'. Four Irish saints, abbots and bishops of the sixth and seventh centuries, bore this name. The greatest of these was Finian of Clonard, (an important school of the period) who taught Columba and other famous figures of the time. Still in use in the Irish community.

S.D. 12th December

Foster The Old English form of the name 'Vedast'. A sixth-century saint who was a co-worker of St Remigius in the conversion of the Franks. His memory is perpetuated in England by a church dedicated to him close to St Paul's in London, and several other medieval churches.

S.D. 6th February

Francis   This is the English form of the Italian 'Francesco', originally meaning 'French' or 'Frenchman'. There are twenty-two saints, all of whom took their name from the famous St Francis of Assisi. His real name was Giovanni but he was nicknamed 'Francesco' because his wealthy father had business connections with the French. A pleasure-seeking youth, Francis (1181–1226) turned his back on wealth and position to lead a life of poverty and humble service of the poor. So many followed his example that in 1209 he founded the Order of Friars Minor; of whom there were 5,000 by 1219. He sent his Friars to preach throughout Europe and especially into the university centres, including Oxford. In September 1224 Francis received a direct vision of Christ and the stigmata of the Passion. He is best remembered for his love of nature, animals and gentle humility.

S.D. 4th October

Frank   Since the sixteenth century this has been the common abbreviation of Francis; however, of Germanic origin it originally referred to a member of the tribe of the Franks from which the country once called Gaul received the name, France.

Fred   Short form of 'Frederick'.

Frederick   A popular European name ('Fredericus' Latin; 'Friedrich' German; 'Federigo' Italian; etc.) it is of Germanic origin and means 'peaceful ruler'. There were two little-known saintly medieval bishops of this name. Once used by the Normans, it was reintroduced into England during Victorian times.

S.D. 27th May

G

Gabriel Hebrew name meaning 'man of God'; the biblical name of the messenger from God, the archangel who appeared to Daniel (Dan. 8:16), Zechariah (Luke 1:19) and, most famously, to Mary the mother of Jesus (Luke 1:26). Three little-known saints took the name, but it has only rarely been used in the English-speaking world.

S.D. 29th September

Geoff Short form of 'Geoffrey'.

Geoffrey (Jeffrey) The modern name, from the Middle English 'Geffrey', originates from two Old Germanic names; meaning 'God's divine peace'. Very popular in medieval England (e.g. Geoffrey Chaucer) it dropped out of favour from the fifteenth to nineteenth centuries, but returned to usage in the twentieth century. There were several little-known medieval saints of this name.

S.D. 25th September

George One of the most European of names ('Georgius' Latin; 'Georges' French; 'Giorgio' Italian; 'Georg' Danish; 'Yuri' Russian; etc.) it originates from the Greek for 'farmer' and came into English via Old French and Latin. There are ten saints of this name, but the most famous is the shadowy patron saint of England who was a Christian martyr (d.c. 300) who suffered under the Emperor

Diocletian at Lydda, Palestine. All other legends, including the dragon story, have been shown to be fictitious. The Crusaders brought veneration of him back to Europe where the name has remained popular.

S.D. 23rd April

Gerald From the Old German 'Gairovald' meaning 'spear-ruler'. It was introduced into England, and subsequently Ireland, by the Normans. Although its usage died out in England it continued to be popular in Ireland. It was reintroduced into England during the nineteenth century. There are seven little-known medieval saints of this name.

S.D. 5th April

Gerard Probably introduced into England by the Normans it is derived from an Old French name of Germanic origins meaning 'spear-brave'. More common in the Middle Ages than 'Gerald', sixteen saintly men bore this name, the best known being the eighteenth-century Gerald Majella who, as a tailor, joined the Redemptorist Order. He was famous for the many and various supernatural phenomena which filled his life. Rarely used now except in the Roman Catholic community.

S.D. 16th October

Gervase (Gervaise) A Norman name of no certain origin, the meaning is sometimes given as 'spear vassal'. The remains of two martyrs (second century) Gervase and Protase, were discovered at Milan in 386, little else is known about them. Not common nowadays, it has occasional use among Roman Catholics.

S.D. 19th June

Gideon   Hebrew name meaning 'destroyer' or 'he who cuts down'; biblical name of the son of Joash (Judg. 6:11) who led the Israelites against the Midianites. Adopted as a Christian name by the seventeenth-century Puritans and still found in the USA.

S.D. 1st September

Gilbert   From the Old German 'Gisilbert' meaning 'bright pledge'. Introduced into England by the Normans it became one of the most popular of Christian names. Of the three saints of this name, Gilbert of Sempringham (Lincolnshire) was the most famous; he founded the only English Religious Order of monks and nuns, called the Gilbertine Order.

S.D. 4th February

Giles   From the Latin and Greek original 'Aegidius' meaning 'young goat'. Very popular in the Latin form 'Egidius' in the Middle Ages, there are over one hundred and sixty churches dedicated to St Giles (there were several but the popular saint was an eighth-century French abbot) who was also patron saint of cripples and beggars.

S.D. 1st September

Godfrey   Meaning 'God's peace' the name comes from the Old German 'Godafrid'. The Normans introduced the name into Britain; it was one of the most popular names in the twelfth and thirteenth centuries. There were several little-known saints, Godfrey of Amiens (1066–1115) being specially regarded. (This name should not be confused with 'Geoffrey'.)

S.D. 8th November

Gregory   From the Latin 'Gregorius' meaning 'the Watchful, or vigilant one', the name has found its way into every European language because of its strong Christian past. A popular name in early Christian times, there are at least twenty-four saints, including two great saintly theologians, Gregory of Nyssa (d.c. 395) and Gregory Nazianzen (d. 389) and the famous Pope, St Gregory the Great (540–604).

S.D. 3rd September

Guy The English form, via the French, of the Latin 'Vitus' or 'Guido' meaning 'life' or 'the guide'. Several little-known medieval saints bore the name. It was introduced into England by the Normans and it remained popular until 'Guy Fawkes'. It came back into use in the nineteenth century.

S.D. 31st March

H

Hadrian (*See Adrian.*)

Harold An Anglo-Saxon name from '*here*' and '*weald*' meaning 'army commander'. Not commonly found during the Middle Ages, although there was St Harold (d. 1168) said to have been murdered at Gloucester. It was revived in the nineteenth century.

S.D. 25th March

Henry One of the most popular of continental names, it originates from the Old German meaning 'lord or ruler of the estate'. Up until the seventeenth century the English version ('Heinrich' German; 'Henri' French; 'Enrico' Italian; etc.) was 'Harry' or 'Herry'. The first St Henry (there are five saints of this name) was Henry the Good (973–1024) the Holy Roman

Emperor, who gave protection to the Church in turbulant times.

S.D. 13th July

Herbert   From the Old German 'Hariberct' meaning 'brilliant warrior'. Popular in Norman times, it went out of use in the late Middle Ages but was reintroduced in the nineteenth century. There are three little-known saints who bore the name.

S.D. 20th August

Hilary   (An ancient masculine name which is now more often given to girls.) It originates from the Latin '*hilarius*' meaning 'cheerful'. The name was popular in the Middle Ages (particularly in France) bestowed in honour of the great theologian, St Hilary of Poitiers (315–68); there are twelve other male saints, including one pope (d. 468).

S.D. 13th January

Hiram   A biblical name (see 2 Sam. 2:11) which is either Hebrew or Phoenician in origin, meaning 'most noble one'. Used by the seventeenth-century Puritans, it soon dropped out of use in England but continues to be bestowed in the USA.

Hubert   From the Old German 'Hugubert' meaning 'bright mind'. It was introduced into England by the Normans and remained popular probably because of devotion to St Hubert, patron of hunters (d. 727). According to a late legend he was converted to Christianity while out hunting.

S.D. 3rd November

Hugh   Of uncertain origin it is probably from the French name 'Hugues' meaning 'bright heart or spirit'. Introduced into England by the Normans, it was popular in medieval England because of a national veneration for St Hugh of Lincoln (1135–1200). There are a further six European saints of this name, the most important being Hugh the Great of Cluny (1024–1109) who ruled over 1,000 monasteries throughout Europe.

S.D. 29th April

Hugo Latin form of 'Hugh', so variant (*see Hugh*).

Humphrey There was an Old English 'Hunfrith', but this appears to have been absorbed into the Norman name of Germanic origin, 'Hunfrid' meaning 'protector of the peace'. There were two little-known saints of this name. Common in medieval England it is associated today with the film star Humphrey Bogart.

S.D. 8th March

I

Ignatius A Latin name derived from the family name 'Egnatius' probably meaning 'fiery patriot'. Christian use derives from the famous St Ignatius of Antioch (d.*c.* 107) whose letters, learning and heroic death in the Roman arena inspired many (a). The name was most popular in Russia and Spain, and there were several Spanish saints, the most important being the founder of the Society of Jesus (Jesuits) St Ignatius of Loyola (1491–1556) (b). In the English-speaking world it is used mainly by Roman Catholics.

(a) S.D. 17th October (b) S.D. 31st July

Immanuel (*See Emanuel.*)

Inigo   The Spanish version of 'Ignatius' (*see Ignatius*).

Ira   From the Hebrew meaning 'watchful'. This is the name of two biblical characters (see 2 Sam. 20:26; 23:26). Apart from the English Puritans of the seventeenth century it has not been used in Britain, but it is still used in the USA.

Isaac   A Hebrew name meaning 'He (God) may laugh', see the story explaining the name (Gen. 18:9ff). Issac was the child promised to the aged Abraham and Sarah and honoured by Jews and Christians as one of the founding Patriarchs of the Chosen People. There are eight saints, mostly of the early years of Christianity. Still used occasionally among Christian Jews (Messianic Jews) it has otherwise dropped out of use.

S.D. 9th September

Isidore   From the Greek meaning 'the gift of Isis'. In spite of its pagan origins the name was very popular in the early centuries of Christianity. There are ten saints in the Christian calendar, the most important being the great writer St Isidore of Seville (*c.* 560–636). Outside of Spain it is regarded as a typically Jewish name and seldom used today.

S.D. 4th April

Ivan   The Russian form of 'John' (*see John*).

Ivor (Ivar)   This probably originates from the Old Norse name 'Ivarr', meaning 'battle archer'; it was borne by several Danish kings of Dublin in the ninth century. It was also the name of a saint who was a contemporary of St Patrick.

S.D. 23rd April

J

Jack Originally a pet form of 'John'; it is now a given name in its own right. It was, at one time, thought to have originated from the French 'Jacques' or the English 'James'; research has shown that this is not the case (*see John*).

Jacob The English version of a Hebrew name which has uncertain origins and meaning. It is usually said to mean 'the heel grabber' or 'supplanter' (see Gen. 27:36) but this is uncertain. The name of one of the greatest figures in the Old Testament, the Patriarch who had twelve sons who gave their names to the twelve tribes of Israel. Two of Christ's Apostles bore this name, the English translators of the New Testament used another English form of the Hebrew name 'James' (via the Latin) but retained 'Jacob' for the Old Testament Patriarch (*see James*). There is a St Jacob of Nisibis, a bishop of the fourth century.

S.D. 15th July

James The English form of the Latin 'Jacomus' a variant of 'Jacobus'; so this is the same name as that borne by two of Christ's Apostles and the Patriarch Jacob of the book of Genesis (*see Jacob*). This is a very European name found in every country; ('Jacques' France; 'Giacomo' Italy; etc.). Its popularity throughout the centuries is confirmed by the large number of saints of this name; seventeen and many blessed martyrs. St James the Greater (Apostle) was the son of Zebedee, brother of John (a). St James the Less was a cousin (some believe brother) of Jesus and, after the resurrection, the first Bishop of Jerusalem (b).

(a) S.D. 25th July (b) S.D. 3rd May

Jared   A Hebrew name meaning 'the descendant' found in the Bible (Gen. 5:18), where he is described as the father of Enoch. Used by the Puritans of the seventeenth century, it enjoyed a brief revival in the 1960s.

Jason   From the Greek meaning 'the healer'; it was borne by the famous figure of Greek mythology, who led the Argonauts. The Christian use originates from the Jason of Acts 17:5–9 who later, according to Greek tradition, converted Corfu to Christianity.

S.D. 12th July

Jasper (Gaspar; Caspar)   The English form of the name 'Gaspar', of Persian origin, meaning 'treasurer', which was attached by tradition to one of the Magi, or wise men, who visited the child Jesus. The Gospel of Matthew does not specify how many Magi there were or their names. These were added by a later tradition, well established by the eleventh century. The name was first used in England in the fourteenth century.

Jed   Originally the shortened form of 'Jedidiah', a biblical name (see 2 Sam. 12:25 where it is an alternative name for King Solomon) but now an accepted name in its own right; from the Hebrew meaning 'friend of God'. Still popular in the USA, the full name was frequently used among the seventeenth-century Puritans in Britain and the USA.

Jeff   Shortened form of 'Jeffrey', now used independently.

Jeffrey   (*See Geoffrey.*)

Jeremiah   From the Hebrew meaning 'exalted by the Lord'; the name of one of the great biblical prophets seventh–sixth century BC. His life and prophecies are found in the book which bears his name. It was much used by the seventeenth-century Puritans; and has been popular in modern times in the English form (*see Jeremy*).

S.D. 1st May

Jeremy   The English form of 'Jeremiah' (*see Jeremiah*).

Jerome   The English version, from the Greek, of 'Hieronymos' meaning 'holy name'. There were several saints of this name, by far the most important being St Jerome (*c.* 341–420) who was variously – secretary to a pope, a hermit living at Bethlehem and a famous biblical scholar and translator of the Bible into Latin (the Vulgate text).

S.D. 30th September

Jesse   This was the name of the father of King David (see 1 Sam. 16); it is from the Hebrew meaning either 'God exists' or 'God's gift'. Rarely used now in the British Isles; from the popular use by the Puritans in the seventeenth century it is still found in the USA.

Jethro   From the Hebrew meaning 'abundance' or 'excellence'. It was the name of Moses' father-in-law, who was a priest of the Kenites (see Exod. 4:18). Popular among the Puritans, the name dropped out of use until there was a revival of interest in the 1970s.

Joachim   A biblical name that probably comes from the Hebrew, 'Johoiachin' (see 2 Kgs 24:8) meaning 'judgment of the Lord'. It was popular in medieval times, and there are several lesser-known saints bearing the name, because of the tradition that this was the name of the father of Mary, the mother of Jesus. This tradition rests only on the apocryphal Gospel of James.

S.D. 26th July

Joel   A common name in the Bible borne by thirteen different figures, the most important being one of the twelve minor prophets. Of Hebrew origin it means 'Yahweh (the Lord) is God'; always popular in the Jewish community it was also used by the seventeenth-century Puritans and is still used in the USA.

S.D. 13th July

John   This is the most perennially popular of names throughout Europe ('Jean' French; 'Hans' German; 'Giovanni' Italian; 'Juan' Spanish; etc.). From the Hebrew meaning 'God is gracious', it was the name of the cousin of Jesus, John the Baptist, and his beloved disciple, John, who is credited with the fourth Gospel. Christian history is littered with famous figures bearing this name; for example, 312 saints, twenty-three popes etc. Great theologians, e.g. John Chrysostom (347–407); influential mystics, e.g. St John of the Cross (1542–91); famous martyrs, e.g. St John Fisher (1469–1535) etc. all bore this popular name.

S.D. 27th December

Johnathan   (*See Jonathan.*)

Johnny   Form of 'John'.

Jolyon   Variant form of 'Julian' used in the Middle Ages (*see Julian*).

Jonathan   A popular biblical name, the most famous bearer being the brave and attractive son of King Saul (see 1 Sam. 14). From the Hebrew 'gift of God' it was not commonly used in Europe until after the Reformation.

Jordan   From the Hebrew name for the principal river of the Holy Land, meaning 'flowing down'. It appears to have an earlier root origin in the Old German 'Jordanes', but crusaders and pilgrims used bottled water from the Jordan (where Christ was baptised) and often named their children after the river. Several medieval holy men, preachers and monks, bore the name.

S.D. (Blessed Jordan of Saxony) 15th February

Joseph   From the Hebrew meaning 'may God add' or 'God shall add'. A very popular name in Israel at the time of Christ, from the Old Testament, the favourite son of Jacob (Gen. 37); there was, for example, Joseph of Arimathea who took the body of Jesus down from the cross and buried it, also the husband of Mary, foster father of Jesus (Matt. 1:20). Hence it was a popular name appearing in all European countries and there have been twenty-seven saints bearing the name.

S.D. (St Joseph, husband of Mary) 19th March

Josh   The short form of 'Joshua' (*see Joshua*).

Joshua   A biblical name, from the Hebrew, meaning 'saviour' or 'God is salvation'. The leader of the Israelites after the death of Moses, who led them into the Promised

Land. (For his story see the biblical book named after him.) The most famous bearer of this name we know by the Greek version, 'Jesus'.

'Joshua' was introduced into England, as a Christian name, after the Reformation. In Spain and South America 'Jesus' has been frequently used, but not in the rest of Europe.

S.D. 1st September

Josiah   The Greek version, 'Josias' is sometimes used. The original is Hebrew meaning 'God heals'. There were two biblical characters (see 2 Kgs 22 and Zech. 6:10) but the most famous English personage was the potter Josiah Wedgewood (1730–95). Popular among eighteenth-century Dissenters it was always more popular in the USA than England.

Judd   This began as a familiar form of 'Jordan' (*see Jordan*) in the Middle Ages but has become a name in its own right.

Jude   Derives from the Hebrew name 'Judah', the name of the fourth son of Jacob and Leah. Its meaning is not clear, some have suggested 'God leads'. Jude is also a variant of 'Judas'. Because of the link with Judas Iscariot who betrayed Jesus it has, until recently, rarely been used as a Christian name. The only St Jude (patron of difficult or hopeless cases) was Judas Thaddaeus, another of Christ's Apostles.

S.D. 28th October

Julian   A very popular name among Christians of the first centuries of Christianity, there are thirty saints, mostly martyrs. Derived from the Latin 'Julianus'. In the late Middle Ages the name was used for both genders and the most famous English bearer is the woman mystic Julian of Norwich (*c.* 1342–1413).

S.D. (St Julian, patron of travellers) 13th February

Julius　Believed to be Greek, but its meaning is uncertain. Adopted as a Roman family name; it was used extensively by the early Christians, there being eight martyred saints of the first three centuries, three popes and a famous Christian writer, Julius Africanus (*c.* 160–240). There is a French version 'Jules'; and the Welsh 'Iolo' is sometimes used.

S.D. St Julius I (Pope) 12th April

Justin　A derivative of the Latin '*justus*' meaning 'the just one'; the English form of the name 'Justinus'. There are seven saints with this name, the most important being Justin Martyr (*c.* 100–165) who argued and wrote to defend the Christian faith; he was beheaded in Rome.

S.D. 1st June

Justus　(*See Justin.*) Another name popular with the early Christians, there are fourteen saints in the Christian calendar. St Justus (d. 627), the third Archbishop of Canterbury, was a Benedictine monk who came from Rome with St Augustine.

S.D. 10th November

K

Kane　From the Irish; it is the English form of the Celtic 'Cathan' meaning 'little warlike one'. There was an obscure Irish saint named St Cathan (sixth century), a bishop in Northern Ireland.

S.D. 17th May

Karl   (*See Carl.*)

Kean (Keane)   The English form of the Celtic name 'Cian' meaning 'bold and handsome'. There was a sixth-century Welsh hermit-saint of this name.

S.D. 11th December

Keenan   A variant of 'Kian' (*see Kean*).

Ken   Short form of 'Kenneth' (*see Kenneth*).

Kenneth   Of Gaelic origin meaning 'the handsome'. There are two little-known saints of this name; the more prominent being a Welsh hermit of the sixth century who lived on the peninsula of Gower.

S.D. 1st August

Kenny   The familiar form of 'Kenneth'; but also a name in its own right. There is a St Kenny who was a sixth-century Irish missionary to Scotland. The town of Kilkenny is named after him.

S.D. 11th October

Kevin   From the Irish 'Coemgen' meaning 'comely' or 'gentle'. St Keven (d.c. 618) was the abbot-founder of the famous Glendalough monastery and, in modern times, one of the patrons of Dublin.

S.D. 3rd June

Kieran (Kieron)   The English form of the Gaelic 'Cieran' which means 'small and dark-skinned'. There are two sixth-century Irish saints of this name; Bishop Kieran has been called 'the first-born of the saints of Ireland'; ordained Bishop of Ossory by St Patrick. The Abbot Keiran founded a monastery at West Meath.

S.D. (St Kieran, bishop) 5th March

Killian (Kilian) From the Gaelic 'Cillian' meaning 'little warlike one'. Three Irish saints of the seventh century have this name; the more famous was a missionary and Bishop of Wurzburg, where he is still honoured.

S.D. 8th July

Kristen This is the Danish form of 'Christian'.

L

Ladislas A Hungarian name of uncertain origins; it was borne by the great Hungarian saint-king (1040–95) who was a national hero (known in Hungary as Laszlo). Also borne by two other East European saints. Found mainly among Polish or East European Christians.

S.D. 27th June

Lambert From the Old German 'Landebert' meaning 'bright land' or 'rich in land'. Brought to England from the twelfth century onwards by Flemish weavers, among whom it was popular because of St Lambert of Maestricht (d. 709), bishop and martyr. There are four other saints of the same name.

S.D. 17th September

Laurence (Lawrence) From the French form of the Latin 'Laurentius' meaning 'person from Laurentum'. This name was very popular in medieval England due to two influences; the popularity of St Laurence who was martyred in Rome in 258 (a) (there are 237 English churches dedicated to him) and St Laurence of Canterbury (d. 619) a respected Archbishop of Canterbury (b). In Ireland the name has been widely used because of St Laurence O'Toole, a reforming bishop of the twelfth century (c). There have been nine other saints of this name.

(a) S.D. 10th August (b) S.D. 2nd February
(c) S.D. 14th November

Leander   This is the Latin form of the Greek name 'Leandros', meaning 'the lion man'. Apart from the Leander of Greek mythology there was a famous Christian saint of the sixth century. He was a friend of St Gregory the Great and a great Bishop of Seville, where he is still honoured.

S.D. 27th February

Len   Short form of 'Leonard' (*see Leonard*).

Leo   From the Greek word for 'lion' via the Latin '*leo*'. It has always been a popular Christian name being borne by fifteen saints and thirteen popes. The most famous pope being St Leo the Great (d. 461). 'Leon' has been quite common in France and this spelling was popular in medieval England. Nowadays it is more often found in the Jewish community.

S.D. 10th November

Leonard   From the Old German 'Leonhard' meaning 'lion brave'; it became a popular French name, due to St Leonard of Noblac (d. 559) whose cult was widespread in Western Europe. The Normans brought the name to England, and 177 English churches were dedicated to St Leonard (and a Sussex town was named after him). The name enjoyed a revival in the nineteenth century.

S.D. 6th November

Leopold   From the Old German 'Leudbald' meaning 'brave for the people'. There is a St Leopold the Good

(1073–1136) but the use of the name in England, from the nineteenth century was more likely because of the popularity of Leopold, King of the Belgians (1790–1865), an uncle of Queen Victoria.

S.D. 15th November

Lewie An alternative spelling of 'Louis' (*see Louis*).

Lewis The usual English form of the French name 'Louis' (*see Louis*).

Lex The short form of 'Alex' (*see Alexis and Alexander*).

Liam Irish form of 'William' (*see William*).

Linus This is the Latin form of the Greek 'Linos' meaning 'flax-coloured hair'. There is a character in Greek mythology, but Christian usage comes from St Linus, the bishop that followed St Peter at Rome (67–79). Modern use is probably inspired by the character in the famous 'Peanuts' strip-cartoon.

S.D. 23rd September

Llewelyn A popular Welsh name derived from the ancient name 'Llywelyn' meaning 'lion like'. There is a sixth-century Welsh saint, monk at Welshpool, of this name.

S.D. 7th April

Lorcan The English form of a Gaelic name; it is also found in English as 'Laurence'. St Lorcan was Laurence O'Toole (*see Laurence*).

Louis Of Frankish origin, this very common French name is found throughout Europe ('Ludovicus' Latin; 'Luigi' Italian; 'Luis' Spanish; 'Ludwig' German;

'Lewis' English; etc.). Before the revolution it was the most popular male forename; eighteen French kings bore the name, one of whom Louis IX (1214–70) was honoured as a saint. There were numerous other saints of the same name. It was introduced into England soon after the Norman Conquest in the form of 'Lewis', which gave rise to a number of related surnames.

S.D. 25th August

Lucas Variant of 'Luke'; used by the translators who produced the Authorized Version of the New Testament (*see Luke*).

Luke From the Latin 'Lucas', but originally a Greek word meaning 'a person from Lucania'. The name of the Gentile doctor from Antioch, who was a friend of St Paul, and writer of the third Gospel and the Acts of the Apostles (a). The name is not found in England before the twelfth century but has been in use since. There are eight other saints including the Englishman, Luke Kirby (b) who was tortured in the Tower of London and died (1582) on Tyburn for his faith.

(a) S.D. 18th October (b) S.D. 30th May

Luther Taken from the surname of the famous theologian and reformer, Martin Luther (1483–1546). Of Old German origin the word means 'famous warrior'. Mostly used in North America, especially after the assassination of the heroic civil rights leader, Martin Luther King (1929–68).

M

Magnus From the Latin for 'great' and was first applied to the Emperor Charlemagne (Carolus Magnus or Charles the Great). It was adopted by the Scandinavians and there were seven Norwegian kings of this name. There are eleven little-known saints who also bore the name.

S.D. (St Magnus of the Orkneys) 16th April

Malachy (Malachi) The English form of the Irish 'Maolmhaodhog'. The original Irish bearer of the name was an Irish king who defeated the Norse invaders. Later chroniclers linked this with the name of the Old Testament prophet, Malachi (Hebrew for 'my messenger'), the last of the twelve minor prophets. Later Christians were more likely named after the famous Irish saint, Malachy O'More (1094–1148) Archbishop of Armagh and energetic reforming churchman.

S.D. 3rd November

Malcolm The English form of the Gaelic name 'Maol-Columb' meaning 'follower, or disciple, of St Columba'. The name 'Columba' means 'dove' (*see Colum*); he was the sixth-century Irish saint who did much to convert the Scots. Hence it has for centuries been a favourite Scottish name; but more widely used in the twentieth century.

Manny The familiar form for 'Emanuel'; used mainly in the Jewish community (*see Emanuel*).

Manuel The Spanish and Portuguese form of 'Emanuel' (*see Emanuel*).

Marc The French form of 'Mark' but gaining in popularity in Britain (*see Mark*).

Marcel French name taken from the Latin name 'Marcellus'. A very popular name with Christians of the first four hundred years of Christianity; there are seventeen saints, including one pope. The French connection is with St Marcellus (d. 274) a Roman missionary to Gaul, who was beheaded there.

S.D. 29th June

Marcus The original Latin form of the English 'Mark', a name of uncertain origins, perhaps from 'Mars' the Roman god of war; so the usual meaning given for the name is 'follower of Mars' (*see Mark*).

Mark From the Latin name 'Marcus' (*see Marcus*). It was borne by the writer of the second Gospel, although scholars believe that Mark was the first to write an account of the 'Good News' (gospel). He is thought to be the 'John Mark' of Mark 14:51–2. According to tradition he founded the Church in Alexandria, where he died a martyr. His body was transferred to Venice in the ninth century. There are twenty other saints of this name, including a pope. In spite of this the name only became widely used in modern times.

S.D. 25th April

Martin The English form of the Latin name 'Martinus', probably derived from the Roman god, Mars; so the name is believed to mean 'warlike' or 'warrior'. This was a very popular name throughout Europe in the Middle Ages and since, due first to the fame of St Martin of Tours (*c.* 316–97) (a) and later, for Protestants, the influence of Martin Luther (1483–1546): added to both of these, in modern times, is the popularity of Martin Luther King (1929–68). Besides numerous saints (another popular saint was St Martin Porres, 1569–1639) (b) there were five popes.

(a) S.D. 11th November (b) S.D. 3rd November

Marty Short form of 'Martin'; but it has been used as a name in its own right.

Martyn Variant spelling of 'Martin'.

Matthew (Mathew) From the Hebrew 'Mattathiah' meaning 'gift of God'. It became 'Matthaeus' or 'Matthias' in Latin. It was introduced into England by the Normans and was very common in the Middle Ages. Hence there are several saints of this name, but the most famous was the evangelist, author of the first Gospel. He was also known as Levi and was originally a tax-collector before being called to follow Christ.

S.D. 21st September

Matthias This is one of the forms of 'Matthew' (*see Matthew*). To distinguish the two Apostles of the same name, the disciple chosen to replace Judas as one of the twelve Apostles was given the alternative name by the translators of the New Testament. Details of his later life are not known.

S.D. 14th May

Maurice From the Latin name 'Mauricius', derived from 'Maurus' meaning 'Moorish-looking' or 'swarthy'. This was the name of a Roman officer and member of the Theban unit of soldiers who refused to worship pagan gods (*c.* 287) and were massacred *en masse* by other, pagan, units, near Agaunum, Switzerland. The name was introduced into Britain by the Normans, and sometimes appears in the form of 'Morris'.

S.D. 22nd September

Max   Short form of 'Maximilian' (*see Maximilian*).

Maximilian   This originates from the combination of two Latin names – 'Maximus' (the greatest) and 'Aemilianus' – so means 'the most excellent'. Borne by three martyrs of the third century, it is famous in the late twentieth century from St Maximilian Kolbe (1894–1941) who rescued Jews in Cracow, Poland, and died heroically for another prisoner in Auschwitz concentration camp. For historical reasons the name has been particularly popular in Germany.

S.D. 14th August

Micah   Hebrew name from 'Micaiah' meaning 'who is like God?' The name of one of the minor prophets, and a book of the Bible coming after the Book of Jonah. Not often used in Britain but occasionally used in the USA.

S.D. 15th January

Michael   The English form of a Hebrew name that comes from the same root as 'Micah' meaning 'who is like God?' The Bible describes the role of the Archangel Michael (Dan. 10:13 and Rev. 12:7) as captain of the heavenly host, so he has been the patron of soldiers. Popular name throughout Europe, there are 687 churches in England dedicated to him; there are eight other lesser-known saints.

S.D. 29th September

Mick   Short form of 'Michael' (*see Michael*).

Mihangel   Old Welsh form of 'Michael' (*see Michael*).

Mike   Short form of 'Michael', sometimes used as an independent name (*see Michael*).

Miles   Introduced into England by the Normans, its antecedents are not clear; it may have come from the Old German 'Milo'. This form of the name was common in the Middle Ages. It could mean 'millstone' from the Greek; or 'soldier' from the Latin. Several saintly persons bore the name Milo, and a Catholic martyr who died at Rochester, 1590, was Miles Gerard.

S.D. 30th April

Milo   Alternative form of 'Miles' (*see Miles*).

Morris   A variant form of 'Maurice' (*see Maurice*) popular in England in the Middle Ages; however, it has developed into a forename in its own right in modern times.

Moses   The English form of the Hebrew name 'Moshe'; it is believed to be of Egyptian origin and said to mean 'taken from the water'; which would fit the story of Moses, the Patriarch who first bore the name (see Exod. 2:10) and who was brought up in the Egyptian Court. He was the great Hebrew leader and lawgiver and founder of Judaism. Although it is now mainly used only in Jewish circles it was popular among English Christians in the seventeenth century. Five early Christian martyrs bore the name.

S.D. 4th September

Moss   Taken from the medieval form of 'Moses' (*see Moses*).

Muirius   The Irish form of 'Maurice' (*see Maurice*).

Mungo   From the Gaelic meaning 'amiable'; it was an epithet applied to St Kentigern and became used occasionally as a Christian name in his native Scotland, especially in the Glasgow area.

S.D. 13th January

Myron   From the Greek '*myron*' or myrrh meaning 'fragrant oil'. Used widely by the early Christians because of its association with one of the gifts brought by the Magi to the child Jesus (see Matt. 2:11). There were two third-century saints, both venerated in the Eastern Church, where the name is more widely used than in the West.

S.D. 17th August

N

Nahum   From the Hebrew meaning 'comforter'. It was the name of one of the minor prophets of the Old Testament, the Book of Nahum has only three chapters and comes after Micah. A popular Jewish name it was often used by seventeenth-century Puritans.

S.D. 1st December

Nat   Short form of 'Nathan' (*see Nathan*).

Nathan   A Hebrew name meaning 'gift of God'. It was the name of an Old Testament prophet who had the courage to challenge King David's immoral behaviour. Six other lesser biblical figures had this name. Mainly used in the Jewish community it has become more widely known in the late twentieth century.

Nathaniel   This is a name from the New Testament, originally from the Hebrew meaning 'God has given'. It was borne by one of Christ's Apostles, who is probably the same person as 'Bartholomew' (John 1:45). Not used in England before the Reformation, it was popular with the Puritans; still occasionally found.

S.D. 24th August

Ned   Short form of 'Edward' (*see Edward*).

Nichol (Nicol)   Short form of 'Nicholas' that was widely used in the Middle Ages (*see 'Nicholas'*).

Nicholas (Nicolas)   From the Latin 'Nicolaus' which in turn comes from the Greek meaning 'victorious leader'. The original St Nicholas (there are twelve saints, including one pope) is one of the most popular of saints in Christendom. His story is almost all legend, excepting the bare facts that he was Bishop of Myra, Lycia, and died *c.* 350. Patron of sailors, pawnbrokers and children; and patron saint of Russia and Greece. His legends suggest great generosity and he has become the 'Santa Claus' (a corruption of his name via the Dutch of New Amsterdam) of the Christmas season.

S.D. 6th December

Nick   Short form of 'Nicholas' (*see Nicholas*).

Nickolas   A variant form of 'Nicholas' (*see Nicholas*).

Ninian   Probably of Celtic origin, its meaning is uncertain. It was the name of a fifth-century (d.*c.* 432) saint who preached Christianity to the Picts in the North of England; he is believed to have been a bishop. Used primarily in Scotland, the name has found wider use in the twentieth century.

S.D. 26th August

Noah Uncertain in origin but believed to be Hebrew meaning 'rest' or 'comfort' (but some suggest 'long-lived'). The story of the biblical character is familiar (see Gen. 5ff) as the good man chosen by God to save his family and representatives of the animal kingdom, to make a fresh start after the great flood. The name has found occasional use since the seventeenth century in Britain and the USA.

Noel The French form of '*natalis*' which is from the Latin '*natalis dies*' referring to the birthday of the Lord, Christmas. Two rather obscure saints bear the name, but it was more likely bestowed on a child born at Christmas time.

S.D. the Christmas season

Noll The familiar form of 'Oliver' (*see Oliver*).

Norbert Of Germanic origin from the words '*nord*' (north) and '*berht*' (bright). There is only one St Norbert (*c.* 1080–1134) who was a German prince who gave up fame and fortune to preach the Gospel. He became the founder of a Religious Order, the Norbertines or Premonstratensians (or White Canons). Many houses were founded throughout Europe, especially in France, Hungary and Britain; famous for their work for religious revival in Europe after the Second World War. The name is more commonly found in the USA than in Britain.

S.D. 6th June

O

Oliver Originates from the French name 'Olivier' which appears to come from the Latin for 'olive tree'. It was a fairly popular name in the Middle Ages due to association with the court of the Emperor Charlemagne. Popular in the Roman Catholic community in modern times because of St Oliver Plunket (1629–81) the Irish bishop who died at Tyburn, London for (the charge read) 'propagating the Catholic religion'.

S.D. 11th July

Ollie Familiar form of 'Oliver' (*see Oliver*).

Omar From the Hebrew meaning 'talkative'. Found in the Bible (see Gen. 36:11) it was used occasionally in Puritan times, but in recent years it has become associated with the Arab community.

Oran (Oren) The English form of the Gaelic 'Odharan' meaning 'sallow'. There is an obscure Irish saint, St Oran of Meath (*c.* 563). The 'Oren' form is found in the Bible in 1 Chronicles. Never much used in Britain, it is found in the USA.

S.D. 22nd October

Osmond (Osmund) From the Old English meaning 'divine protector'. It was in general use in England before the Norman Conquest but taken up by the Normans. There was just the one St Osmond; he was appointed Bishop of Salisbury in 1072 where he finished the cathedral. Not much used in modern times.

S.D. 4th December

Oswald   From the Old English 'Osweald' meaning 'divinely powerful'. There were two English saints of this name. The first was the seventh-century King of Northumbria (a); the second was an Archbishop of York (d. 922) (b). Popular in the Middle Ages, the name dropped out of use but returned to be occasionally used in the nineteenth century.

(a) S.D. 5th August (b) S.D. 28th February

Otto   The modern German form of 'Odo', which means 'wealthy, prosperous man'. There were two saints of this name; the better known is Otto of Bamberg (1062–1139) a German missionary and bishop.

S.D. 2nd July

Owen   A common Welsh name although its origin and meaning is uncertain. There are two, rather obscure saints of this name, both of the seventh century.

S.D. 4th March

P

Paddy   The familiar shortened form of 'Patrick' (*see Patrick*).

Padraig   The Irish form of 'Patrick' (*see Patrick*).

Patrick   From the Latin '*patricius*' meaning 'nobleman'. This was the name adopted by a Christian Briton named Sucat when he was consecrated as a missionary to Ireland, where he had been enslaved as a youth. St Patrick (*c*. 390–461) established the Catholic Church in Ireland. Many legends surround his life; however, he did found the See of Armagh and his hard work and sanctity earnt him the title 'Apostle of Ireland'.

There are three more little-known saints in the Christian calendar of the same name.

S.D. 17th March

Paul   From the Latin for 'small'. This is a widely used name in all Christian countries ('Paolo' Italian and Portuguese; 'Pablo' Spanish; 'Pavel' Russian; etc.). This was the name Saul of Tarsus took after his experience on the Damascus road and conversion, before his great missionary journies. He endured many hardships and his thirteen letters to the communities that he founded were accepted by the Church as inspired Scripture. Interestingly this name is more popular in England in the twentieth century than it was throughout the whole of the Middle Ages. There have been thirty-nine saints named after the Apostle to the Gentiles and six popes.

S.D. 29th June

Peter   The Latin name 'Petrus' comes from the Greek 'Petros' which is a translation of the Aramaic 'Cephas' (demonstrating how Christ's teaching went from Aramaic to Greek and then into Latin) which means 'stone' or 'rock'. This was the nickname that Jesus gave to Simon Bar Jona, whom Christ chose as leader of the Twelve Apostles and later became the first Bishop of Rome. This has been one of the most popular male forenames in history; it is prominent in all European countries. In England there are 1,140 churches dedicated to St Peter. The most common form in the Middle Ages was 'Piers'; at the Reformation it dropped out of use, because of its association with Rome and the Papacy. It returned to use in the twentieth century. There are seventy-four other saints who took their name from the leader of the Apostles.

S.D. 29th June

Phil   Short form of 'Philip' (*see Philip*).

Philip   From the Greek meaning 'lover of horses'. As a Greek name it was popular in the Greek period. It appears four times in the Bible; in the New Testament it is the name of one of Christ's Apostles, who came from Bethsaida and died a martyr's death in Phrygia (a). It is also the name of one of the seven deacons chosen to help the Apostles (see Acts 6:5; 8:26) (b). A popular name throughout the centuries (there are sixteen more saints) and throughout Europe. In England St Philip Howard (d. 1595) is honoured at Arundel for dying for his Catholic faith in the Tower of London (c).

(a) S.D. 3rd May (b) S.D. 6th June (c) S.D. 19th October

Phineas   From the Greek meaning 'mouth of brass'; it is found three times in the Old Testament, borne by minor characters, e.g. Aaron's grandson (Num. 25:6–15). This was a popular name among the seventeenth-century Puritans and remains popular in some parts of the USA.

Piers   The medieval form of 'Peter' (*see Peter*).

Q

Quentin   From the Latin word for 'fifth'. The French town of St Quentin was named after a Roman missionary to Northern France who was martyred there *c.* 287. The name was brought to England by the Normans.

S.D. 31st October

Quintin (Quinton)   Variant forms of Quentin (*see Quentin*).

R

Ralph Originally from the Old Norse, via the Normans, the English name is more commonly found in its French form of 'Raoul', meaning 'wolf counsel'. A popular name, as 'Ralf' in Tudor times, there are several saintly martyrs of that period, particularly St Ralph Sherwin (d. 1581) and a ninth-century Benedictine saint.

S.D. 21st June

Ray The short form of 'Raymond' (*see Raymond*).

Raymond (Raymund) From the Old German 'Raginmund' meaning 'wise protection'. A very popular European name in the twelfth–fourteenth centuries, when the six saints of this name lived, the most famous being St Raymund of Penafort, a famous Spanish preacher. The Normans brought the name to England.

S.D. 7th January

Reg Shortened form of 'Reginald' (*see Reginald*).

Reginald From the Old English 'Regenweald', meaning 'mighty power'. Three saintly monks bore this name, although it is derived from Reynold (*see Reynold*).

S.D. 1st February

Reuben A biblical name from the Hebrew meaning 'behold the son'. This was the name of one of Jacob's sons (Gen. 30:14) and the name of one of the twelve tribes of Israel. Steadily popular as a Jewish name, it enjoyed Christian usage in the seventeenth century and again in the nineteenth; but not currently.

Reynold   The Old English 'Regenweald' ('mighty power') combined, after the Norman Conquest, with the Old French 'Reinald', to produce a name which was popular in Norman England.

Richard   An Old French name, derived from Frankish roots, meaning 'powerful one'; it was imported into England by the Normans. It has enjoyed continual popularity in England from the Norman Conquest to today. This included the folk hero, King Richard the Lionheart (1157–99) but also the saintly Bishop of Chichester, Richard de Wych (1197–1253), and the English mystic, Richard Rolle (1300–49).

S.D. 3rd April

Richie   A familiar form of 'Richard' (*see Richard*).

Ricky   A familiar form of 'Richard' (*see Richard*).

Robert   A popular English name derived from the French meaning 'bright and shining fame', and imported by the Normans. (It was the name of William the Conqueror's father.) There are nine medieval saints of this name and the famous Jesuit intellectual, St Robert Bellarmine (1542–1621). Many surnames and nicknames (e.g. 'Rob', 'Bob', 'Nob' and 'Robin') have been derived over the centuries from Robert.

S.D. 17th September

Roderick   Derived from the Old German 'Hrodric' meaning 'famous wealthy ruler'. Introduced into England by the Normans it did not survive the Middle Ages and was reintroduced in the nineteenth century. There is only one obscure saint of this name.

S.D. 13th March

Roger The name emerged from a blending of the Old English 'Hrothgar' and, at the Norman Conquest, the French 'Roger'; meaning 'famous spearman'. It was a popular name throughout the Middle Ages and gave rise to many surnames. There are several saintly personages of this name; all rather obscure.

S.D. 15th November

Ronald Originally the Scottish equivalent of 'Reginald' meaning 'mighty power'. St Ronald (d. 1158) was a chieftain of Orkney who built the cathedral of St Magnus at Kirkwall. He died a martyr's death.

S.D. 20th August

Rowan It is the English version of the Gaelic name 'Ruadhan', meaning 'little brown one'. It was borne by a little-known saint of the sixth century who founded the monastery at Lothra. (The name can be used for male or female.)

S

St John (Pronounced 'sin-jen'.) Obviously a name originating from St John; either the Evangelist or the Baptist. Mainly in use in Roman Catholic circles this century.

S.D. 24th June

Sam Short form of 'Samuel' (*see Samuel*).

Samson (Sampson) From the Hebrew 'Shimshon' meaning 'sun child'. It was the name of the famous Jewish champion and judge (see the Book of Judges 13–16 for his story). It was also the name of two sixth-century saints. The most well-known was Abbot of Caldey

Island who became one of the greatest missionaries of his period; he is still revered in Wales and Brittany.

S.D. 28th July

Samuel   This is the English form of the Hebrew name 'Shemuel', probably meaning 'God has listened'. The name of one of the greatest of the Hebrew prophets (eleventh century BC) who anointed Saul as King; his story can be found in two books of the Bible that the Reformed tradition have named after him (they are known as the First and Second Books of Kings in the Orthodox and Roman Catholic traditions).

The name entered popular use after the Reformation.

S.D. 20th August

Seamas (Seamus)   The Irish form of 'James' (*see James*).

Sean   The Irish form of 'John' (*see John*).

Sebastian   From the Latin 'Sebastianus' meaning 'man from Sebaste'. It was the name of one of the most renowned of the Roman martyrs. According to unreliable sources, Sebastian was an officer in the imperial army of Diocletian, when he converted to Christianity the Emperor handed him over to fellow officers to fire their arrows at (*c.* 288). His sufferings have been a favourite subject for many artists over the centuries.

S.D. 20th January

Seumas (Seumus)   Scottish Gaelic form of 'James' (*see James*).

Shamus   The English spelling sometimes adopted for the Irish 'Seamas'.

Shaun   The English spelling of the Irish 'Sean'.

Silas   A Greek name, a short form of 'Silouanus' meaning 'from the forest'. It was the name of one of St Paul's travelling companions (see Acts 15:22; 18:5). Legend has it that he became the first Bishop of Corinth. The name was not used in England before the Reformation.

S.D. 13th July

Silvester (Sylvester)   From the Latin meaning 'woody' or 'growing in a wood'. There were five saints of this name, the most important being Pope Silvester (d. 335) who was the first to govern the Western Church free of persecution.

S.D. 31st December

Simeon   A biblical name, from the Hebrew 'Shimeon' meaning 'one who hears'. A common name in Israel there are several biblical figures, particularly (see Luke 2:25) the elderly 'just and devout' Jew who blessed the child Jesus in the temple. There are ten other saints of this name, mostly hermits, the most renowned being Simeon Stylites – there is an elder (390–459) and a younger one (521–97). Both amazingly lived a hermit existence on top of a stone pillar.

S.D. 5th January

Simon   This is the more usual English form of 'Simeon' (*see Simeon*). There are seven saints of this name; apart from Simon who became 'Peter', from an English point of view the most famous would be St Simon Stock (1165–1265) who was one of the first Englishmen to join the Order of Carmelites. He established the Order in England, particularly Oxford (1253) and Cambridge (1248). His relics are at the Carmelite Friary, Aylesford, Kent.

S.D. 16th May

Stan   Short form of 'Stanislaus' or 'Stanley' (*see Stanislaus*).

Stanislaus   This is a Slavic name meaning 'stand for glory'. It was the name of two famous Polish saints; the first (1030–79) was rather like Thomas Becket, murdered in church while at Mass for opposing the Polish king (a). The second, Stanislaus Kostka (1550–68) died as a young Jesuit (b). The name is popular in Polish circles, whether in Poland or in Britain.

(a) S.D. 11th April (b) S.D. 13th November

Stephen   This is the English variant of the Graeco-Latin name 'Stephanus' meaning 'the crowned one'. It is one of the most European of names ('Stefano' Italian; 'Etienne' French; 'Esteban' Spanish; 'Istvan' Hungarian; etc.) and one of the most popular of male Christian names throughout the centuries. Its Christian usage springs from the deacon Stephen (see Acts 6–7) who was the first Christian martyr. There have been over thirty further saints of the same name, including a saintly King of Hungary (*c.* 935–1038) and a pope.

S.D. (St Stephen martyr) 26th December

Steven   A variant of 'Stephen' (*see Stephen*).

T

Ted (Teddy)   Short form of 'Edward' (*see Edward*) or 'Theodore' (*see Theodore*).

Terence   From the Latin name 'Terentius', which is of uncertain origin and meaning. There were several little-known saints bearing this name in the early centuries of Christianity. Not much used except in Ireland.

S.D. 21st June

Theo   Short form of 'Theodore' (*see Theodore*).

Theodore   From the Greek name 'Theodoros' meaning 'gift of God'. This was a very popular name in Christianity for the first thousand years of its history. There were twenty-nine saints, which included, early martyrs, an Archbishop of Canterbury (*c.* 602–90) and St Theodore Studites (759–826) a famous monastic leader of the Eastern Church.

Thomas   From an Aramaic word meaning 'twin'; in the Gospels it is the name of one of the twelve Apostles. It became one of the most popular of male names, perhaps because the doubts of the Apostle Thomas made him seem human and approachable (a). There were sixty saintly men of this name, including the great theologian Thomas Aquinas (1225–74) (b), the martyred Archbishop of Canterbury, Thomas Becket (1118–70) (c), and the chancellor of England who opposed King Henry VIII, Thomas More (1478–1535) (d). At the height of its popularity in Tudor times the name was shortened to 'Thome', and later 'Tom'. (It was so popular that British soldiers in the First World War were nicknamed 'Tommies'.)

(a) S.D. 3rd July
(b) S.D. 28th January
(c) S.D. 28th December
(d) S.D. 22nd June

Timothy   This is the English form of the Greek name 'Timotheos' meaning 'honouring God'. It was the name of the Apostle Paul's convert who became a travelling companion, and to whom Paul addressed two letters (see 1 and 2 Timothy). Although there were eight early Christian saints of this name, it was not used in the English-speaking world until well after the Reformation.

S.D. 26th January

Tobias (Toby)   From the Hebrew name 'Tobiah' meaning 'God is good'. It is the name of several biblical characters but particularly the hero of the deutero-canonical Book of Tobit. The story of Tobias and the angel was popular in the Middle Ages. There was also a fourth-century martyr of this name.

S.D. 2nd November

Tony   Shortened form of 'Antony' or 'Anthony' (*see Antony*).

V

Valentine   From the Latin and derived from '*valens*' meaning 'strong'. There were probably six saints of this name, all from the first centuries of Christianity, and all quite obscure. The martyr who is celebrated on 14th February had been a priest and a doctor and died in Rome in 269.

The custom of sending 'Valentines' on 14th February is based on the medieval belief that birds begin to pair on that day.

S.D. 14th February

Vic   Short form of 'Victor' (*see Victor*).

Victor   From the Latin word '*victor*' meaning 'conqueror'. A very popular name among the early Christians; there were over thirty saints, including the first African pope (d. 198) and Victor III (1027–87) who had been a successful Benedictine Abbot of Monte Cassino. Rare in the Middle Ages, the name was popular in France after the Revolution.

S.D. 16th September

Vincent   Taken from the Latin name 'Vincentius' derived from '*vincens*' meaning 'conquering'. There are twenty-four saints who bore this name, of whom two are famous: Vincent de Paul (1581–1660) renowned for his works of charity for the needy, and founder of the Sisters of Charity (a); Vincent Ferrer (1350–1419) a famous preacher (b).

(a) S.D. 27th September
(b) S.D. 5th April

Virgil   This name is more frequently found in the USA. The original Latin name, meaning 'staff bearer', was 'Vergilius'. There was a renowned Latin poet of this name but the Christian usage sprang from three saints.

S.D. 26th June

Vivian   This originates from the Latin name 'Vivianus' meaning 'lively one'. There were three little-known saints of this name. In the Middle Ages the name was sometimes spelt 'Fithian'.

S.D. 28th August

W

Walter From the Old German word 'Waldhar' meaning 'mighty warrior'. The Normans introduced the name into England and it was very popular in medieval times. There have been five saints with this name.

S.D. 4th June

Wesley Taken from the surname of the founder of Methodism, John Wesley (1703–91), also his brother Charles Wesley (1707–88) who was a great hymn writer. At first the name was only used in Methodist circles, but it is now used widely without reference to its religious origins.

Wilfrid (Wilfred) An Old English name arising from the compound of *'will'* (will) and *'frith'* (peace) so 'strong peacemaker'. There were two eighth century Anglo-Saxon saints of this name; the better-known (whose name may have been Waldfridus) played a leading role at the important Synod of Whitby (664) and spread the gospel among the Frisians and South Saxons. Not so often used now, the name was very popular in the nineteenth century and early part of the twentieth century.

S.D. 12th October

Will Short form of 'William' (*see William*).

William From the Old German 'Willahelm' meaning 'determined protector'. It was introduced into England by the Normans and quickly became one of the commonest male names in England. A truly European name it is found throughout Europe ('Gulielmus' Latin; 'Guillaum' French; 'Guillermo' Spanish;

'Gulielmo' Italian; etc.). There were over forty-five saintly men, mostly in the medieval period, but none were particularly well-known.

S.D. (St William of York) 8th June

X

Xavier Of uncertain origin, possibly Spanish with Arabic antecedents, meaning 'bright'. It was the surname of the Spanish saint, Francis Xavier, one of the first members of the Society of Jesus (Jesuits) and an amazing missionary in the East who is believed to have converted, before modern times, more people to Christianity than anyone else. The name is used almost exclusively in the Roman Catholic community.

S.D. 3rd December

GIRLS' NAMES

A

Abbie   Shortened form of 'Abigail' (*see Abigail*).

Abigail   From the Hebrew meaning 'father rejoiced'. In the Bible it was the name of the wife of Nabal (1 Sam. 25:3) who became one of King David's wives. David's second sister (2 Sam. 17:25) also bore this name. Popular in seventeenth-century England it went out of fashion because it became the slang term for a lady's maid. Often shortened to 'Abbey' or 'Gail'.

Ada   Originally from the Old German meaning 'prosperous and joyful', it arrived in England in the eighteenth-century from Germany and was very popular in the nineteenth century. There was a St Ada, a seventh-century Abbess of Saint-Julien-des-Pres, Mans. It has been used as a shortened form of 'Adelaide' or 'Adele'.

S.D. 4th December

Adelaide   Of Germanic origin meaning 'noble and kind'. The popularity of William IV's queen led to its general use in England in the nineteenth century. There were three saints of this name, the most influential being the widow of the Holy Roman Emperor, Otto the Great (*c.* 930–99) who became regent and was revered for her sanctity. (Often shortened to 'Addy' or 'Ada'.)

S.D. 16th December

Adeline   Introduced into England by the Normans it originates from the Old German meaning 'noble woman'. In common use in the Middle Ages, there are two little-known saints of that period; one, a French abbess, being the granddaughter of William the Conqueror.

S.D. 20th October

Agatha From the Latin form of the Greek name 'Agathe' meaning 'good'. This was the name of a very famous and popular virgin-martyr, from Palermo, Sicily, of the third century, honoured in both the Eastern and Western Church. Hence a form of the name is found in every European country. (Often abbreviated to 'Aggy'.)

S.D. 5th February

Agnes The Latin version of the Greek name 'Hagne' meaning 'pure'. St Agnes, a fourth-century virgin-martyr, was very popular throughout Christian Europe in the Middle Ages so the name is found in every country ('Agnes' French; 'Agnese' Italian; 'Inez' Spanish; etc.). There are four later saints of the same name. From the twelfth to sixteenth-century it was one of the most common names used in England for girls.

S.D. 21st January

Aileen (*See Eileen.*)

Aimee From the French '*aimer*' meaning 'to love'. So originally it was a nickname meaning 'beloved'. There is, however, a male saint with this name; a seventh-century French abbot.

S.D. 13th September

Alberta The female form of 'Albert'. (*See Albert.*)

Albina (Albinia) Derived from the Latin word '*albus*' meaning 'white'. Common in Italy the name was first used in England in the sixteenth century. Not often used in the twentieth century it originates from a St Albina, a young virgin-martyr of the third century.

S.D. 16th December

Alex (Alexa)   The female form of 'Alexander' (*see Alexander*).

Alexandra (Alexandria)   (*See Alexander.*)

Alexia   The female form of 'Alexis' (*see Alexis*).

Alice   From the Old French and a variant of 'Adelaide'. In the twelfth century in France and England it was appearing as 'Alicia' or 'Alesia'. It dropped out of use in seventeenth-century England, but was revived by Romance writers in the nineteenth century (*see Adelaide*).

Alicia (Alesia)   (*See Alice.*)

Alison   In thirteenth-century France it was a familiar form of 'Alice' (*see Alice*).

Anastasia   From the Russian, and a popular name in Eastern Europe. It is derived from the Greek male name 'Anastasios' which comes from the Greek for 'resurrection'. There are twenty-seven male saints of the name 'Anastasius', including two popes. Of the four female saints, the most famous is the fourth-century martyr who died at Sirmium in Dalmatia.

S.D. 25th December

Andrea   The female form of 'Andrew' (*see Andrew*).

Angel   Until recently this has been an exclusively male name (e.g. 'Angelo' is a common male name in Italy). It comes from the Greek word '*angelos*' which in the

New Testament meant 'messenger from God'. There are several little-known male saints of this name. Through its female use in the American Black community it has entered England, in recent years, as a female name.

S.D. 5th May

Angela The original female form of the male name 'Angel' or 'Angelus' (*see Angel*). There was a famous St Angela de' Merici (1474–1540) who devoted her life to the education of girls. This led to the foundation of the first Roman Catholic teaching Order (1535), the Ursulines, specially dedicated to the education of girls.

S.D. 27th January

Angelica Derived from the Latin, feminine form of 'Angelus' (*see Angel and Angela*).

Angelina A variant form of 'Angela' or 'Angelica' (*see Angela*).

Angie Familiar form of 'Angela' (*see Angela*).

Anita From the Spanish form ('Ana') of 'Ann' (*see Ann*).

Ann (Anna, Anne) From the Hebrew 'Hanna' (*see Hannah*). This was the name according to tradition (not recorded in the Bible) of the mother of the Virgin Mary. It was the great popularity of this 'saint' in the Middle Ages, throughout the whole of Europe, that made it such a popular name in all European countries.

S.D. 26th July

Annie Familiar form of 'Ann' (*see Ann*).

Annette   In France, the familiar form of 'Ann'. It has become a name this century in its own right in the English speaking world (*see Ann*).

Antoinette   This is the French, feminine form, of 'Antoine', in English 'Anthony' (*see Antony*).

Antonia   This is the Italian, feminine form, of 'Antony' (*see Antony*). There were two fifteenth-century saintly Italian women of this name; (a) Antonia of Florence and (b) Antonia of Brescia.

(a) S.D. 28th February (b) S.D. 27th October

Ariadne   From the Greek meaning 'holy one'. In Greek mythology she was the daughter of the Cretan king, Minos, who helped Theseus to escape the labyrinth. The name survived into Christian times because of St Ariadne, who died in Phrygia for her faith in AD 130.

S.D. 17th September

Audrey   From the Anglo-Saxon and is derived from the Old English name 'Etheldreda' meaning 'strong and noble' (*see Etheldreda*).

Audrina   A variant of 'Audrey' (*see Etheldreda*).

Augusta   The feminine form of 'Augustus' or 'Augustine'. From the Latin meaning 'sacred and majestic' (*see Augustine*). There was a virgin-martyr (fifth century) of this name.

S.D. 27th March

Aurelia   From the Latin word '*aureus*' meaning 'golden'. It was a Roman family name and also the name of three little-known saints of early Christianity. Unknown in medieval England, although used in

France, the name was revived in the seventeenth century.

S.D. 15th October

Ava Probably from the German; the meaning is uncertain. There was a ninth-century saint, niece of the great King Pepin, who became Abbess of Denain in Hainault. Modern popularity probably springs from the film star, Ava Gardner.

S.D. 29th April

Averil (Avril) From the Old English meaning 'slayer of the boar'. Used throughout the Middle Ages, it was the name of a little-known, fifth-century, Yorkshire saint.

B

Barbara A popular European name (e.g. 'Barbe' French; 'Varvara' Russian; etc.). From the Greek for 'strange' or 'foreign'. St Barbara, a third-century Syrian virgin-martyr, was highly regarded in the Middle Ages but modern research casts doubts upon her existence. Legend has it that for her faith she was shut up in a tower and later killed by her father. He was struck by lightning. As a result Barbara became patron saint of firework-makers and protectress against lightning and fire.

S.D. 4th December

Bea Short form of 'Beatrice' or 'Beatrix' (*see Beatrix*).

Beatrice This is the French and Italian form of 'Beatrix' (*see Beatrix*).

Beatrix   From the Latin meaning 'bringer of joy'. It was a popular name throughout Europe during the Middle Ages (e.g. 'Beatrice' French; 'Beatrice' Italian; 'Beatriz' Spanish). There were several saintly women of this name, particularly the fourth-century Roman martyr and the fifteenth-century Portuguese Abbess of Toledo. The name went out of fashion in the seventeenth century, but was revived again in the nineteenth.

S.D. 16th August

Becca   Short form of 'Rebecca' (*see Rebecca*).

Becky   Short form of 'Rebecca' (*see Rebecca*).

Bella   Shortened form of 'Isabella' (*see Isabella*).

Benedicta   From the Latin '*benedictus*' meaning 'blessed'. It is the feminine version of 'Benedict' (*see Benedict*). This male name was very common throughout medieval Christian Europe, consequently there are five, rather obscure, female saints with the name 'Benedicta'.

S.D. 17th August

Bernadette   This is the French feminine diminutive form of 'Bernard' (*see Bernard*). Mostly used by members of the Roman Catholic Community in honour of St Bernadette of Lourdes (1844–79), the young French girl who had a series of visions of the Virgin Mary at Lourdes.

S.D. 16th April

Bernice   This is the modern version of 'Berenice'. It comes from the Greek and means 'bringer of victory'. The name is found in Acts 25:13; she is the sister of King

Agrippa and later mistress of the Emperor Titus. It was also borne by a little-known fourth-century Syrian martyr. The name was first used by the Puritans in England.

S.D. 4th October

Bertha From the Latin version of the Frankish name meaning 'bright and shining'. Not in fashion now it was in regular use during the Middle Ages. Three saints bore the name, the most interesting being the sixth-century daughter of the King of the Franks who became the first Christian queen in England. As Queen of Kent she welcomed the missionary St Augustine to Canterbury.

S.D. 24th March

Bess Short form of 'Elizabeth' (*see Elizabeth*).

Beth Short form of 'Elizabeth' (*see Elizabeth*).

Bethany One of the very few modern Christian names to come into vogue. It is taken from the place in the New Testament (John 11:1;12:1), a village just outside Jerusalem, where Lazarus, Martha and Mary lived; and where Jesus stayed during Holy Week. It is from the Hebrew and probably means 'house of figs'.

Betty Short form of 'Elizabeth' (*see Elizabeth*).

Beulah From the Hebrew meaning 'the married one'. It is a biblical name applied by the prophet Isaiah to the land of Israel (Isa. 62:4). It was adopted by the Puritans in the seventeenth century when they were seeking new names to avoid using the traditional saints' names.

Bianca From the Italian '*bianca*' meaning 'white'; it is a variant form of 'Blanche' (*see Blanche*).

Biddy The short form, used mainly in Ireland, for 'Bridget' (*see Bridget*).

Blanche From the French, being the feminine of the adjective '*blanc*' meaning 'white'. Introduced into England by the Normans the name was more commonly used in its Latin form 'Candida' (*see Candida*). There were eight saints of this name; that of most interest was the Devon saint (no firm dates) whose original shrine, surviving the Reformation, is found in the church and village named after her, Whit(e)church, Devon.

S.D. 1st June

Brenda Originating from the Shetland Isles it is probably the feminine form of the Norse name 'Brand' meaning 'fiery'. However, in Ireland where it has been popular, it has been used as the female version of 'Brendan'. He was one of the three most famous saints in Ireland (*see Brendan*).

S.D. 16th May

Bride A short form of 'Bridget' (*see Bridget*).

Bridget The English form, via the French 'Brigette', of the Irish 'Brighid'; later 'Brigit' or 'Brigid'. Originally it was the name of an ancient Celtic goddess (meaning 'the high or exalted one') but it became a very common name in Ireland and England because of the popularity of St Bridget (*c.* 450–525) the second patron of Ireland. (There is also a fourteenth-century St Bridget of Sweden.) She founded the first Religious House (convent) for women in Ireland. Her popularity in medieval England is attested by the part of the City of London, Bridewell, named after her.

S.D. 1st February

Brigitte (Brigette) The French form of 'Bridget' (*see Bridget*).

Britt The Swedish form of 'Bridget' (*see Bridget*).

C

Caitlin (Caitrin) The Gaelic form of 'Catherine' (*see Catherine*).

Candace From the Latin '*canditia*' meaning 'whiteness' or 'pure'. Originally it was a dynastic title of the queens of Ethiopia. The name is found in the New Testament, referring to an Ethiopian queen in Acts 8:27 when the deacon, Philip, baptises her eunuch.

Candice An alternative spelling of 'Candace' (*see Candace*).

Candida From the Latin meaning 'white'. The name also appears in its French form 'Blanche' (*see Blanche*). One of the eight saints who bore this name was, according to legend, an aged woman who in 78 welcomed St Peter to Naples on his way to Rome and was healed by him.

S.D. 4th September

Carla Feminine form of 'Carl' (*see Carl*).

Carlotta The Italian form of 'Charlotte' (*see Charlotte*).

Carmel From the Hebrew meaning 'garden'. It is the name of a mountain near Haifa in Israel, inhabited from early Christian times by hermits. These hermits were eventually organised into the Carmelite Order. 'Our

Lady of Carmel' is an ancient title given to the Virgin Mary; there is a church dedicated to her on the mountain. The name is chiefly found in the Roman Catholic community.

Carmela Variant form of 'Carmel' (*see Carmel*).

Carmen The Spanish form of 'Carmel' (*see Carmel*).

Carol The English version of 'Carolus', Latin for 'Charles'. It probably started as a short form of 'Caroline', also derived from 'Carolus' (*see Charles*).

Carole The French form of 'Carol' (*see Carol*).

Caroline From the Italian feminine form of 'Charles'. Introduced into England by George II's queen, Caroline of Brandenburg; hence it was a popular name in eighteenth-century England (*see Charles*).

Carolyn Variant form of 'Caroline' (*see Caroline*).

Cath Shortened form of 'Catherine' (*see Catherine*).

Catherine (Catharine) Variant form, originally spelt 'Katherine' (*see Katherine*) from the Latin 'Katerina' and later 'Katharina', derived from the Greek word 'katharos' meaning 'pure'. There are eight saints of this name witnessing to its popularity in the Middle Ages. Little is known about the original St Catherine (a), an early virgin-martyr of Alexandria, except the legend that she was tortured on a spiked wheel (the origin of the firework called the Catherine wheel). A more important figure was St Catherine of Siena (b) the fourteenth-century intellectual reformer who is patron saint of Italy.

(a) S.D. 25th November (b) S.D. 29th April

Cathleen   A variant spelling of 'Kathleen' (*see Kathleen*).

Cathy   Familiar form of 'Catherine' (*see Catherine*).

Catrin   The Welsh form of 'Catherine' (*see Catherine*).

Cecilia   A popular European name (e.g. 'Cecile' French; 'Cacile' German) throughout history, it originates from the Latin 'Caecilia', the feminine of 'Caecilius' (*see Cecil*). The name acquires its fame from the second–third century Roman virgin-martyr who is, for no accountable reason, the patroness of music. The name was introduced into England by the Normans; William the Conqueror had a daughter of the name.

S.D. 22nd November

Celeste   From the Latin '*caelestis*' meaning 'heavenly'; the name was more common in France than elsewhere. It was used by the early Christians but there is no well-known saint of this name.

Chantal   A French name originating from the popularity in France of St Jane Francis de Chantal (a place in Saône-et-Loire). As a widow, under the guidance of St Francis de Sales, she founded the new Religious Order of the Visitation and had sixty-six convents under her guidance at her death (1572–1641).

S.D. 12th December

Chantel (Chantelle)   Alternative spellings of 'Chantal' (*see Chantal*).

Charis   From the Greek 'kharis' meaning 'grace'. The idea of God's grace was central to the teaching of the New Testament, but it was not used as a name until after the Reformation. It first appears in the seventeenth century. It has been reinforced in the latter part of the twentieth century due to renewed Christian interest in the charisms bestowed by God and the Charismatic Renewal movement.

Charissa   A variant of 'Charis' (see Charis).

Charity   It comes from the French 'charité', but originally from the Latin 'caritas', meaning 'love' or 'charity'. Its use as a name was inspired by St Paul's description of love in 1 Corinthians 13. It appeared after the Reformation and was popular in Victorian times (sometimes contracted to 'Cherry').

Charlene (Charline)   A modern name found mostly in Australia and the USA, from the male 'Charles' with the feminine suffix (see Charles).

Charlotte   Originally from the Italian 'Carlotta', being the feminine version of 'Carlo' (Charles). Not used in England before the seventeenth century, it became common due to the popularity of Queen Charlotte (1744–1818), the wife of George III (see Charles).

Cherry   Familiar form of 'Charity' (see Charity).

Chloe   From the Greek 'khloe' meaning 'fresh young blossom'. Not used until the time of the seventeenth-century Puritans who having destroyed any figures or pictures of the saints found in English parish churches, refused to use their names for their children. Instead they searched the New Testament for fresh names. They found a passing reference to a certain 'Chloe' in 1 Corinthians 1:11 and a new Christian name came into usage. It has remained more popular than most names introduced at that time.

Chiara The Italian form of 'Clare' or 'Clara' (*see Clare*).

Chris Short form of 'Christine' and associated names (*see Christine*).

Christa The Latin short form of 'Christine' (*see Christine*).

Christabel Although it occurs in the seventeenth century, derived from 'Christine' with suffix '-bel', its popularity appears to spring from Coleridge's poem 'Christabel' (1816) (*see Christine*).

Christene A variant form of 'Christine' (*see Christine*).

Christiana (Christianna) The femine form of 'Christian' (see Christian).

Christina From the Latin feminine form of 'Christianus' (*see Christian*). There are five saints of this name; none of them well-known. All were virgins; two died for their faith and the remainder were saintly nuns.

S.D. 24th July

Christine From the French form of 'Christina', which, in turn is from the Latin 'Christianus' meaning 'Christian'. It was not much used in England before the end of the nineteenth century.

Cicely A variant form of 'Cecily' which is derived from 'Cecilia' (*see Cecilia*).

Claire   The French form of 'Clara' or 'Clare'. The Normans introduced it into England, but it went out of use. It was revived in the nineteenth century (*see Clare*).

Clara   From the feminine of the Latin word '*clarus*' meaning 'bright' or 'clear'. Its use in thirteenth-century England sprang from the existence of six saints of the name 'Clarus', all early and all associated with France (e.g. St Clair, a town in Normandy). The English version 'Clare' became more common.

S.D. 4th November

Clare   The English form of 'Clara' (the Italian 'Chiara'). In later Christian times it became very popular because of the devotion and honour given to St Clare of Assisi (*c.* 1194–1253), the influential friend of St Francis of Assisi. Inspired by Francis she was as devoted to the poor as he was and founded the Religious Order of the Poor Clares. She governed the Order for forty years and was consulted by popes, cardinals and bishops.

S.D. 11th August

Clarice (Clarisse, Clarissa)   A French derivative of 'Clara' which was in use in England as early as 1199 and continued to be bestowed throughout the twelfth and thirteenth centuries (*see Clara and Clare*).

Claudia   From the feminine of the Latin name 'Claudius' (*see Claude*) meaning 'lame'. The name appears among a group of Christian converts of St Paul in 2 Timothy 4:21. It was used by the Puritans in the seventeenth century in their campaign to rid the country of traditional names and find new biblical names to use for their children. There were also two early Christian martyrs of this name.

S.D. 7th August

Claudine From the French feminine diminutive form of 'Claude' (*see Claude*).

Clemence (Clemency) From the Latin '*clementia*' meaning 'mildness'. It appears to have been used as the feminine form of the male name 'Clement' (*see Clement*).

Clementina (Clementine) Further feminine forms of 'Clement'. First used in the nineteenth century and gained in popularity, but rarely found in the twentieth century.

Colette Originates from the French name 'Nicolette' which is the diminutive of 'Nicole', the French feminine form of 'Nicholas' (*see Nicholas*). There is a St Colette (originally Nicolette Boilet, 1381–1447) famous for reforming the Poor Clares' Order and helping St Vincent Ferrer to resolve the Papal Schism.

S.D. 6th March

Columbine From the Italian 'Colombina', which comes from '*columba*' meaning 'dove'. It can be regarded as the feminine of the male name 'Columba', from St Columba, the famous Scottish saint of the sixth century (*see Columba*). However, the modern use of the name springs from a nineteenth-century practice of coining new female names from flowers and nature. The columbine is a flower of the aquilegia family with five spurred petals.

S.D. 9th June

Connie Familiar form of 'Constance' (*see Constance*).

Constance   The English form of the Latin word '*constantia*' meaning 'constancy'. Also the feminine of the male name 'Constantius' or 'Constantine'. Introduced into England by the Normans, it was common throughout the Middle Ages. There were several saints with the name 'Constantine', the most important being the emperor who died in 337 and one first-century martyr named 'Constantia', who died with a St Felix at Nocera, Italy.

S.D. 19th September

Consuelo   From the Spanish for 'counsel', from the title of the Virgin Mary, 'Our Lady of Good Counsel'. Used in Spanish-speaking parts of America and occasionally in the Roman Catholic community in Britain.

Cornelia   From the Latin; the feminine form of 'Cornelius' (*see Cornelius*). There are two saintly women of this name; a martyr who, in the third century, died with Theodulus in North Africa. In the nineteenth century the American nun, Cornelia Connelly, who founded the public school for girls at Mayfield, East Sussex.

S.D. 31st March

Cristina   The form of 'Christina' found in Spain, Italy and Portugal (*see Christina*).

D

Damaris   A Greek name found in the Acts of the Apostles (17:34), an Athenian woman convert of St Paul. Its meaning is not certain. This was one of the names discovered in the Bible by the seventeenth-century Puritans and adopted by them. Very occasionally found in the twentieth century.

Daniela   From the Latin form, the feminine of 'Daniel' (*see Daniel*).

Danielle   From the French feminine form of 'Daniel' (*see Daniel*).

Daria   The feminine form of the male 'Darius' (not now in use). There was a St Daria who died at Rome for her Christian faith (283) with her Egyptian husband, Chrysanthus; they are buried on the Via Salaria.

S.D. 25th October

Davina (Davinia)   The feminine form of 'David' originating from Scotland (*see David*). It could also be the feminine form of 'Davinus'; the saint of this name was an Armenian who died in 1051 at Lucca, Italy.

S.D. 3rd June

Deborah   From the Hebrew for 'bee'. It was the name of one of the great female figures of the Old Testament, the judge and prophetess (Judg. 4–5). It was also the name of Rebecca's nurse (Gen. 35:8). Always a popular Jewish name it was adopted by the seventeenth-century Puritans. It has retained its popularity and is usually shortened to 'Debbie' or 'Debra' which have become name in their own right.

Delilah   A biblical name but its origins are uncertain. It is given the meaning 'gentle temptress' from the actions of the Delilah who tempted Samson (Judg. 16:4–20). It was the seventeenth-century Puritans who introduced the name to England; but it is rarely used in the late twentieth century.

Delores   A variant form of 'Dolores' (*see Dolores*).

Delphine   French name taken from the Latin 'Delphina' meaning 'woman from Delphi'. There was a rather obscure St Delphinus, a fifth-century Bishop of Bordeaux; and a fourteenth-century saintly noblewoman, Delphina, from Languedoc.

S.D. 9th December

Denise   Originally from the Latin 'Dionysia', this is the French feminine form of 'Dennis' (*see Dennis*).

Desiree   French name taken from the Latin '*desiderata*' meaning 'desired'. In early Christian times it was given to a child who had been longed-for. There are four male saints of the name 'Desideratus', none of them well-known.

S.D. 8th May

Diana   From the Latin name of the moon goddess, the equivalent of the Greek goddess, Artemis. The name appears in Acts 19:24–41 when St Paul becomes involved in riots stirred up by worshippers of Diana of the Ephesians. It was not considered suitable as a Christian name, and does not appear in common use until after the sixteenth century. However, there was a twelfth-century saintly Dominican nun, of Bologna, of this name. The French form 'Diane' has become well-established in the twentieth century.

S.D. 10th June

Diane   (*See Diana.*)

Dina   (*See Dinah.*)

Dinah   From the Hebrew meaning 'judgment'. In the Bible she is the daughter of Jacob by Leah (Gen. 34). Not used until the seventeenth century it was then very popular until the nineteenth century. In modern times it is sometimes confused with 'Diana'.

Dolores A Spanish name taken from the title of the Virgin Mary, 'Maria de los Dolores' meaning 'Mary of the Sorrows'. An ancient devotion to the Seven Sorrows of the Virgin Mary was formalised by the Roman Catholic Church when it instituted (1423) a feast day for 'Our Lady of Sorrows' on 15th September. Widely used in the English-speaking world, particularly among American Roman Catholics.

S.D. 15th September

Dominica From the Latin, the feminine form of 'Dominic' (*see Dominic*).

Dominique The French feminine form of 'Dominic' (*see Dominic*).

Donna A modern name, originating from the USA, not in use until the late 1920s. It comes from the Madonna, a title given to the Virgin Mary, particularly in Italian/Spanish communities.

Dorcas From the Greek '*dorkas*' meaning 'gazelle' or 'graceful'. It was used by the early Christians because of the good widow of Joppa (also known as 'Tabitha') raised to life by Paul (see Acts 9:32–43). It dropped out of use in the Middle Ages but was enthusiastically revived by the seventeenth-century Puritans.

S.D. 25th October

Doris From the Greek meaning 'from the sea'. It appears in Greek mythology as the name of a minor goddess of the sea. There were several, very obscure, early

Christian martyrs of this name; however, the name only really came into use in the nineteenth century.

Dorothea The feminine form of the male Latin name 'Dorotheus' meaning 'gift of God'. There were five male saints, all before the eleventh century, of this name, and three female saints, the best known being the virgin-martyr who died (*c*. 300) under the Emperor Diocletian at Caesarea.

S.D. 6th February

Dorothy The English form of 'Dorothea' (*see Dorothea*).

Drusilla From the Latin meaning 'the strong one'. It was the name of one of St Paul's converts, the wife of the Roman citizen, Felix (Acts 24:24). The Puritans of the seventeenth century, in their drive to find new biblical names for their children, were the first to use it.

Dymphna This is the English version of the Irish 'Damhnait' of uncertain meaning. Very little is known about the Irish virgin-saint of this name. As many cases of epilepsy and insanity were cured at her shrine in Belgium she became patroness of the mentally ill.

S.D. 15th May

E

Edith From the Old English 'Eadgyth' coming from the two words '*ead*' (riches) and '*gyth*' (war). It was a popular Saxon name, which survived the Norman Conquest, with two saints, Edith of Polesworth (d. 925) and Edith of Wilton (961–84) the daughter of King Edgar. In the twentieth century there was St

Edith Stein (1891–1942) the Polish Carmelite sister who died heroically in Auschwitz.

S.D. (St Edith Stein) 9th August

Edna　From the Hebrew meaning 'pleasure' it is found in the apocryphal books of the Bible as the wife of Enoch and in the Book of Tobit, as the mother of Sarah (7:15). It appears to have come into England in the eighteenth century from Ireland, where it has been more commonly found.

Edwina　The modern female form of 'Edwin' (*see Edwin*).

Eileen (Aileen)　An Irish name that became popular in England at the beginning of the twentieth century. It is thought to be the Irish equivalent of Helen, but may have evolved from 'Evelyn' (*see Helen*).

Elaine　An Old French form of 'Helen'. As an independent name it is found in the fifteenth-century legend of King Arthur (*Morte D'Arthur*) by Thomas Malory but there is no evidence of common use before the nineteenth century.

Eleanor　From the Old French 'Alienor' and always thought to be a form of 'Helen', although this is now questioned. Introduced into England by Eleanor of Aquitaine (1122–1204) wife of Henry II, the name is found with various spellings (e.g. 'Elinor'; 'Elianor'; etc.). (*See Helen.*)

Elena　The Spanish and Italian form of 'Helen' (*see Helen*).

Eleonora　The Italian form of 'Eleanor' (*see Eleanor*).

Elfreda (Elfleda)   This is the later form of two Old English names, with no clear modern meaning. There were three saints, all pre-Conquest Benedictine nuns, of this name. It was also the name of one of King Alfred's daughters. The name went out of use but was revived in the nineteenth century.

S.D. 8th February

Elisabeth   Alternative spelling of 'Elizabeth' (*see Elizabeth*).

Elise   The French short form of 'Elizabeth' (*see Elizabeth*).

Eliza   Short form of 'Elizabeth' first used in the sixteenth century (*see Elizabeth*).

Elizabeth   From the Hebrew 'Elisheba' meaning 'consecrated to God'. It was the name of Aaron's wife (Exod. 6:23) and more famously the mother of St John the Baptist (Luke 1:60) (a). A popular name throughout Europe, it is usually spelt with a 'z' in England and an 's' throughout the Continent. There have been five saints bearing this name; the most influential being St Elizabeth of Hungary (1207–31) (b). Of interest is St Elizabeth Seton (c) (1774–1821) the first American saint, renown for her work for Catholic schools.

(a) S.D. 5th November (b) S.D. 17th November
(c) S.D. 4th January

Ellen   This was originally a variant of 'Helen' (*see Helen*).

Elsa   A shortened form of 'Elizabeth' (*see Elizabeth*).

Elspeth (Elsie)   The Scottish shortened form of 'Elizabeth' (*see Elizabeth*).

Emily From the Latin name 'Aemilius', it evolved into its present form due to Teutonic influences; meaning 'industrious'. There are three French saints of this name, all nuns; not well known outside of France.

S.D. 17th June

Emma From the Old German meaning 'one who heals'. It was popular among the Normans and became common in England partly because it was the name of the mother of the King, St Edward the Confessor. It was well used throughout the Middle Ages often spelt as 'Emm'. There are several little-known saints of this name, sometimes identified as 'Gemma'.

S.D. 29th June

Erica The feminine form of 'Eric' (*see Eric*).

Esther In the book of the Bible of this name, 'Esther' is said to be a Persian name, the equivalent of the Hebrew 'Hadassah' (Esther 2:7), the meaning is not clear, 'myrtle' and 'star' have both been suggested. Heroine of the Jewish people, Esther saved the Jews from a 'holocaust' planned by the Persian counsellor Haman. Not found in England before the seventeenth century, its use has spread beyond the Jewish community in the twentieth century.

Ethel From the Old English, which originated from the Teutonic, meaning 'noble', it is the shortened form of the old traditional names 'Ethelburga' (a), 'Etheldreda' (b) or 'Ethelfleda' (c). These were all Anglo-Saxon saints, all noblewomen who founded convents in East Anglia and the South-East of England. It was revived, in this short form, in the nineteenth century.

(a) S.D. 5th April (b) S.D. 23rd June (c) S.D. 23rd October

Etta   Short form of 'Henrietta' or 'Rosetta' (*see Henrietta and Rosetta*).

Eugenia   The feminine form of 'Eugene' (*see Eugene*).

Eunice   From the Greek '*eunike*', a compound of two Greek words, meaning 'good victory' or 'victorious'. It was the name of the mother of Paul's disciple, Timothy (Acts 16:1; 2 Tim. 1:5). Not found in medieval times, it was introduced by the Puritans of the seventeenth century keen to avoid using the traditional names of accepted saints.

Eva   The Latin form of 'Eve' (*see Eve*).

Evangeline   A modern name, apparently invented by the American poet Longfellow (1848) derived from the Greek word '*euangeilon*' or the Latin '*evangelium*' meaning 'good news' or 'gospel'. Hence the four Gospel writers are called the 'evangelists'. Common in the USA and occasionally found in Britain.

Eve   The English form of the Latin 'Eva', which comes from the Hebrew 'Havva' (meaning 'living') being the name of the first woman created by God from the rib of Adam (Gen. 2:22). It has been used in England since the thirteenth century.

F

Faith   First used after the Reformation for both boys and girls. It obviously refers to that virtue or quality of believing and trusting in God. It was very popular among the Puritans.

Felicia   The Latin female form of 'Felix' (*see Felix*).

Felicity   The English form of the Latin name 'Felicitas', meaning 'happiness'. A popular feminine name among the early Christians there at least five martyrs of this name during the first centuries of Roman persecution.

S.D. 23rd November

Flora   From the Latin '*flos*' for 'flower' and the Roman goddess of flowers. It appears to have come into England from Scotland in the eighteenth century, through the reputation of Flora MacDonald who helped Bonnie Prince Charles to escape in 1746. Three virgin-martyrs of early Christianity bore the name.

S.D. 24th November

Florence   From the Latin masculine name 'Florentius' which is derived from '*florens*' meaning 'blooming' or 'flourishing'. It was a popular male name, (there are eighteen saintly bishops, abbots and martyrs) but gradually became exclusively a feminine name, perhaps influenced by Florence Nightingale (1820–1910) who was named after the Italian city where she was born.

S.D. 20th June

Frances   The feminine form of Francis. Originally used for both men and women it did not become distinctly feminine until the seventeenth century. There are two famous saints of this name; St Frances of Rome (1384–1440), patron saint of motorists (a); St Frances Xavier Cabrini (1850–1917) foundress of a missionary Order (b). (*See Francis.*)

(a) S.D. 9th March (b) S.D. 22nd December

Francesca The Italian form of 'Frances' (*see Frances*).

Francine From the French familiar form of 'Frances' (*see Frances*).

Freda Short form of various names ending in '-freda' e.g. 'Elfreda'.

Frederica The Latin feminine form of 'Frederick' (*see Frederick*).

G

Gabriela The Latin feminine form of 'Gabriel' (*see Gabriel*).

Gabrielle The French feminine form of 'Gabriel' (*see Gabriel*).

Gemma From the Italian '*gemma*' meaning 'a gem'. From the Italian community the name spread into wider Roman Catholic use because of St Gemma Galgani, a modern saint (1878–1903) who during a short, but very hard, life had many religious experiences including the stigmata. Widely found in the late twentieth century.

S.D. 11th April

Genette Variant spelling of 'Jeanette' (*see Jeanette*).

Genevieve A French name derived from 'Genovefa'; its meaning is uncertain. St Genevieve (422–500) is the patron of Paris. When the city was occupied by the Franks and threatened by Attila and his Huns, Genevieve roused the people to defend their city. The name was first used in Britain in the nineteenth century.

S.D. 3rd January

Georgette   The French feminine name taken from 'Georges', the French for 'George' (see George).

Georgia   From the Latin form of 'George'. There was a St Georgia, (d.c. 500) a French virgin-recluse who lived near Clermont in Auvergene.

                                            S.D. 15th February

Georgiana   From the Latin form of 'George' (see George).

Georgina   The feminine form of 'George' which became popular in eighteenth-century England when the male name was common (see George).

Geraldine   The feminine form of 'Gerald'. It appears to have been invented by the poet Surrey about 1540 in praise of Lady Elizabeth Fitzgerald (see Gerald).

Germaine   The feminine form of the French name 'Germain', which originates from the Latin 'germanus' meaning 'brother'. There are fifteen male saints of this name; the one female St Germaine Cousins (c. 1579–1601) was the daughter of a poor farmer who heroically lived a very harsh life near Toulouse, France.

                                            S.D. 15th June

Gertrude   From the Old German 'Geredrudis' meaning 'spear maiden'. It was the name of one of the Valkyries in the Nordic myths; it was borne by three saints, the most important being St Gertrude the Great (c. 1256–1302), who had many religious experiences and whose writings on Christian mysticism were very influential. Popular in the nineteenth century it is rarely found in the late twentieth century.

                            S.D. (St Gertrude the Great) 16th November

Gillian   The popular English form of 'Julian(na)'. Commonly found in the Middle Ages the two spellings became separate names in the seventeenth century (*see Julian*).

Gina   The short form of 'Georgina' (*see George*).

Giselle   The French form of 'Gisela' which originates from the German word '*gisl*' meaning 'pledge'. St Gisela (d. 1095) was the first Queen of Hungary, wife of St Stephen and sister of St Henry, Emperor of Germany.

S.D. 7th May

Grace   From the Latin '*gracia*' meaning 'grace'. Like 'Faith', 'Hope' and 'Charity' it was introduced after the Reformation and was popular with the Puritans who were trying to avoid using saints' names. They were probably unaware that there are two, little-known, saints who bore the name.

S.D. 5th July

Gwen   The short form of the Welsh name 'Gwendolen' (*see Gwendolen*).

Gwendolen   A Welsh name meaning 'white-browed girl'. There are various spellings for this ancient name; there are two fifth-century saints, and three a little later. It appears to have come into use in England in the nineteenth century.

S.D. 18th October

H

Hannah   From the Hebrew '*hanna*' meaning 'full of grace'. It was the name of the mother of the prophet Samuel

(1 Sam 1:2). The Greek form of the name 'Anna' (*see Ann*) became well-established and widely used throughout Europe. It was the Puritans of the seventeenth-century who revived the original form of the name.

Harriet The English version of the French name 'Henriette' which is the feminine form of 'Henry' (*see Henry*). It first appeared in seventeenth-century France and became popular in England the following century.

Helen The English form of the Greek 'Helene', probably from the Greek word '*helios*' ('sun' or 'light'). The name of the famous beauty of classical legend, Helen of Troy, but widely used throughout Christian Europe, in many and varied forms, because of St Helena, mother of the first Christian Emperor Constantine (*c.* 250–330). She is credited with building many churches in the Holy Land and the discovery of the cross of Christ. Popular from early times in Celtic countries, the traditional English form was 'Ellen'; the current spelling became more popular after the sixteenth century.

S.D. 18th August

Helena The Latin form of 'Helen' (*see Helen*).

Henrietta The Latin form of the French name 'Henriette', which is the feminine form of 'Henry' (*see Henry*).

Hilary (Hillary) Originally, and for centuries, a male name it comes from the Latin '*hilaris*' meaning 'cheerful' (we have the word 'hilarious'). There are thirteen saints (all male) including a pope (d. 468) and a famous theologian, St Hilary of Poitiers (315–68).

S.D. 13th January

Hilda   Originally from Germany, the Old English form was 'Hild', probably derived from the *'hild'* meaning 'war' or 'battle'. It was borne by the influential Northumbrian St Hilda of Whitby (614–80) who convened the important Synod of Whitby which decided the future of the English Church. She has been hailed 'one of the greatest Englishwomen of all time'.

S.D. 17th November

Hope   From 'faith, hope and charity' the fundamental virtues of Christianity. The name was introduced by the Puritans in the seventeenth century. Originally used for both genders, now used only as a girl's name.

Hyacinth   The English form of the Greek name 'Hyakinthos', the name of a flower. Until the nineteenth century it was always a male name; there are five male saints, four of them early martyrs, the fifth was St Hyacinth (1185–1257) given the title 'Apostle of Poland' for his missionary work there.

S.D. 17th August

I

Ida   From the Old German meaning 'work'. It was brought to England by the Normans, ceased to be used about the fourteenth century and revived in the nineteenth. There are seven little-known saintly women of this name.

S.D. 4th September

Imelda   From the Greek meaning 'longed for'. Found in its Latin form in use in Italy and Spain, rarely in Britain.

There was a saintly Imelda Lambertini of Bologna (d. 1333).

S.D. 12th May

Irene From the Greek for 'peace'. A common Byzantine name, it was borne by three martyrs of the fourth century and an empress (d. 803). It first appeared in England in the nineteenth century and grew in popularity in the twentieth.

S.D. 5th April

Isabel (Isobel) Originally the Spanish form of 'Elizabeth'. Interchangeable up to the sixteenth century, it had been, throughout the Middle Ages, one of the most popular feminine names, perhaps because it was the name of three English queens. (*See Elizabeth*.)

Isidora (Isadora) The feminine form of 'Isidore' (*see Isidore*).

Ita Irish name meaning 'desire for truth'. In popular veneration in Ireland St Ita (d.*c*. 570) ranks second to St Bridget; many legends exist but little reliable information.

S.D. 15th January

J

Jacklyn (Jaclyn) Short form of 'Jacquelyn' (*see Jacquelyn*).

Jacqueline The French feminine of 'Jacques' (James) (*see James*). Probably introduced into England from Flanders; from the thirteenth to the seventeenth century it is found in a variety of forms, e.g. 'Jacklin'.

Jacquelyn Variant form of 'Jacqueline' (*see Jacqueline*).

Jan Short form of 'Janet' or 'Janice' (*see Janet*).

Jane The usual modern form of 'Joanna' (Joan) and the English feminine form of 'John'. Widely found throughout Europe (e.g. 'Giovanna' Italian; 'Juana' Spanish; 'Jeanne' French; etc.). Very common in the nineteenth century, it did not appear until the sixteenth century and nowadays is often used in a combination name, e.g. 'Mary-Jane' etc. There are six saints, all of them foundresses of Religious Orders, e.g. St Jane of Valois (1461–1504) who founded the Order of the Annunciation (a) and St Jane-Frances de Chantal (1572–1641) the Visitation Sisters (b).

(a) S.D. 4th February (b) S.D. 12th December

Janelle A modern form of 'Jane' (*see Jane*).

Janet A diminutive form of 'Jane' (*see Jane*).

Janette A modern variant of 'Jane' (*see Jane*).

Janice (Janis) A modern variant, from the USA, of 'Jane' (*see Jane*).

Jayne A variant spelling of 'Jane' (*see Jane*).

Jean Derived from the Old French 'Jehane' (as are 'Jane' and 'Joan') and a feminine form of 'John' (*see John*). It was, at first, solely found in Scotland; in the twentieth century it has become more widely used.

Jemima (Jemina) From the Hebrew meaning 'dove'. In the Bible it was the name of Job's eldest daughter (Job 42:14). It does not appear to have been used until the seventeenth century.

Jemma A variant spelling of 'Gemma' (*see Gemma*).

Joan The usual feminine form of 'John', from the Old French 'Jehane' or the Latin 'Iohanna' (*see John*). Used throughout the Middle Ages, in the sixteenth century it was the third most common feminine name in England. Although there is a 'Joanna' mentioned in the New Testament, Luke 8:3, the famous saint of this name is St Joan of Arc (1412–31).

S.D. 30th May

Joanna From the Greek spelling of the Hebrew name 'Johanna' and in biblical times it was used for men or women (cf. Luke 3:27 and Luke 24:10). Throughout Europe, during the Middle Ages, 'Johanna' was the common feminine form of 'John', this became 'Joanna' and then 'Joan' (*see Joan*).

Johanna (*See Joanna*.)

Joni A modern version of 'Joannie', a familiar form of 'Joan' (*see Joan*).

Josephine From the French, it is the feminine form of 'Joseph' (*see Joseph*).

Joy From the Old French '*joie*' translating the Latin '*gaudia*', which figures so much in Christian spirituality and thought (in the medieval European Christian calendar one day was known as 'Gaudete Sunday'). Used by the seventeenth-century Puritans; the name went out of fashion until the nineteenth century when it reappeared.

Joyce This was a popular medieval name, used for boys and girls, and appears in England from Norman times; in the Norman form 'Josce' meaning 'lord', or the Old English 'Jose'. A highly regarded Breton hermit-saint of the seventh-century made the name popular. It ceased to be a male name about the fourteenth century.

S.D. 13th December

Judith From the Hebrew meaning 'woman from Judea' or 'Jewess'. It was the name of the Jewish heroine who tricked and slew Holofernes, the Assyrian general. The story is found in the Book of Judith in the Apocrypha of the Bible. There was a little-known ninth-century saint of this name. Not in common use in England before the eighteenth-century it has enjoyed popularity since.

S.D. 29th June

Julia The feminine form of 'Julius'. It is found throughout Europe (e.g. 'Julie' French; 'Giulia' Italian; etc.) although it did not appear in common use until the sixteenth century. St Paul in his Letter to the Romans (16:15) refers to a follower of this name and there are seven early Christian martyrs. There is also St Julia Billart (1751–1816) the foundress of the schools and Sisters of Notre Dame.

S.D. 8th April

Juliana The feminine form of 'Julianus'. A popular name in early Christian times, there are seven martyrs, and between the thirteenth and the fifteenth centuries it was one of the most common names; there are four saintly women from this period, including the famous Juliana of Norwich (d. 1423) one of the most celebrated of English mystics (*see Julian*).

S.D. 13th May

Julie The French form of 'Julia' (*see Julia*).

Juliet   The English form of the French name 'Juliette', which is the diminutive of 'Julia' (*see Julia*).

Justina (Justine)   The feminine form of 'Justin' (*see Justin*).

K

Karen (Karin)   The Danish form of 'Katherine'. Introduced into the USA, and thence to Britain, by Scandinavian immigrants (*see Katherine*).

Katarina   The Swedish form of 'Katherine' (*see Katherine*).

Katerina   The Russian form of 'Katherine' (*see Katherine*).

Katherine (Katharine)   The English alternative spelling (*see Catherine*) of the Greek name 'Aikaterine', the meaning of which is thought to be 'pure'.

Kathleen   From 'Caitlin', the Irish version of 'Catherine' (*see Catherine*).

Katya   The familiar form of the Russian 'Yekaterina' (Katherine) (*see Katherine*).

Keren   From the Hebrew meaning 'horn of eye-paint'. It is a shortened form of the name borne by Job's youngest daughter 'Keren-Happuch' (Job 42:14).

Kirsten   The Scandinavian form of 'Christine' (*see Christine*).

Kristen   The Danish form of 'Christine' (*see Christine*).

Kristina   The Swedish form of 'Christine' (*see Christine*).

L

Laura The feminine form of the Latin name 'Laurus' meaning 'laurel'; or possibly the feminine form of 'Laurence'. There was a St Laura, a ninth-century Spanish nun martyred by the Moors. The name probably came into Britain from Italy and was rarely used before the nineteenth century.

S.D. 19th October

Lauren (Loren) A modern name; a feminine form of 'Laurence' (*see Laurence*).

Leah From the Hebrew meaning 'the weary one'. It was the name of the sister of Rachel (Gen. 29:16–35) who was married off to Jacob by Laban. It was first used by the seventeenth-century Puritans as a Christian name.

Lena A shortened form of 'Helena' (*see Helen*).

Leonora A shortened form of 'Eleonora' (*see Eleonora*).

Lilian (Lillian) The origin is uncertain but it is generally believed to be derived from 'Elizabeth' (*see Elizabeth*).

Lois Probably a Greek name, its origins and meaning are unknown. It was the name of the grandmother of Timothy, mentioned in 2 Timothy 1:5. It was adopted by the seventeenth-century Puritans, when they refused to use traditional names for their children.

Lola Originally a Spanish short form of 'Dolores' (*see Dolores*).

Lora   The German form of 'Laura' (*see Laura*).

Loreto   Mainly found in the Roman Catholic community; it is inspired by devotion to the Virgin Mary, under the title 'Our Lady of Loreto'. The place is a town in Italy where legend has it, in the thirteenth century, the house of the Holy Family of Nazareth was transported by angels.

Loretta   A variant form of 'Loreto' (*see Loreto*).

Louisa   The Latin feminine form of 'Louis'. Sometimes used as an alternative spelling of 'Louise' (*see Louise*).

Louise   The French feminine form of 'Louis' (*see Louis*). There is a famous French saint of this name. St Louise de Marillac (1591–1660) a widow who became a nun; she helped St Vincent de Paul to found the Sisters of Charity (1638). Not used in Britain before the seventeenth century, by the end of the twentieth it has become one of the most common baptismal names.

S.D. 15th March

Lucia   The Latin feminine form of 'Lucius' meaning 'light'. There are eighteen little-known saints of early Christian times, with the name 'Lucius'; five female saints named 'Lucia' (or 'Lucy') the most famous being the Sicilian virgin-martyr St Lucy of Syracuse (d. 304) (a). The most modern is Lucy, a Chinese school-teacher beheaded at Kuy-tszheu, in 1862, for her Christian faith (b).

(a) S.D. 13th December (b) S.D. 19th February

Lucilla   A Latin familiar form of 'Lucia' (*see Lucia*). There was a third-century Roman martyr of this name.

S.D. 25th August

Lucy   The modern form of 'Lucia' from the Old French 'Lucie' (*see Lucia*).

Ludmilla (Ludmila)   From a Slavonic name meaning 'beloved of the people'. It originates from Eastern European countries where it comes from St Ludmilla (d. 921) the Duchess of Bohemia, who educated the young St Wenceslaus, and was murdered.

S.D. 16th September

Lydia   From the Greek meaning 'cultured one' or 'woman from Lydia'. According to Acts 16:14 St Lydia, from Thyatira (now Ak-Hissar), was 'a dealer in purple cloth' and St Paul's first European convert. The name was first used in England in the seventeenth century.

S.D. 3rd August

M

Madelaine (Medeleine, Madeline)   From the Hebrew meaning 'woman of Magdala' (a village on the shores of the Sea of Galilee). The English form comes from the French 'Madeleine' referring to Mary Magdalen; in all four Gospels she is portrayed as one of the most devoted followers of Christ. Several little-known saints were named after Mary of Magdala.

S.D. 22nd July

Madelyn   A variant form of 'Madelaine' (*see Madelaine*).

Madoline   A variant form of 'Madelaine' (*see Madelaine*).

Madonna   A modern name originating from the Italian title of the Virgin Mary, meaning 'my lady', and used of, for example, Renaissance paintings and sculptures of the Virgin Mary. It appeared first among the Italian families settled in the USA. Made popular by the 1980s' pop star, Madonna Ciccone.

Magdalen   (*See Madelaine.*)

Mair   The Welsh form of 'Mary' (*see Mary*).

Maire   The Irish form of 'Mary' (*see Mary*).

Mairead   The Irish form of 'Margaret' (*see Margaret*).

Maisie   The Scottish familiar form, derived from 'Mairead', of 'Margaret' (*see Margaret*).

Manuela   From the Spanish feminine form of 'Emanuel' (*see Emanuel*) meaning 'God with us'.

Marcella   The feminine form of the Latin name 'Marcellus', of which there are three saints, including one pope. The name originally meant 'belonging to Mars' (the god, not the planet). There are two saints of this name, the better-known was a saintly widow of Rome (325–410) tortured by the Goths.

S.D. 31st January

Marcia   The feminine form of 'Mark', from the Latin name 'Marcus'. There were three early Christian martyrs of this name, about which little is known (*see Mark*).

Margaret   The English form has come from the French 'Marguerite', which comes from the Latin; however, the name originally appears to be Persian; meaning 'pearl'. It was one of the most widely used feminine names throughout Europe and popular in England since the Norman Conquest. The first St Margaret (called 'Marina' in the Eastern Church) was beheaded at Antioch in the third century for her faith; there were eight further saints, including the famous St Margaret of Scotland (*c.* 1045–93) (a), St Margaret Mary Alacoque (1647–90) (b) and St Margaret Clitherow (1556–86) (c).

(a) S.D. 16th November (b) S.D. 16th October
(c) S.D. 21st October

Margery The common medieval form of 'Margaret' (*see Margaret*).

Marguerite The French form of 'Margaret' (*see Margaret*). There is one saint, Marguerite Bourjeoys (1620–1700) the French-born nun who founded the Sisters of Notre Dame de Montreal and their schools, which spread extensively in the USA.

S.D. 19th January

Maria The Latin form of 'Mary' (*see Mary*).

Marian A variant spelling of 'Marion' (*see Marion*).

Marianne An extending spelling of 'Marian'; thought of as a combination of 'Mary' and 'Ann', but not originally so.

Marie The French form of 'Mary'. Usually pronounced with the emphasis on the end of the word, in the French fashion; sometimes with the accent on the first syllable. (*See Mary.*)

Mariella An Italian form of 'Maria' (*see Mary*).

Marietta An Italian form of 'Maria' (*see Mary*).

Marilyn A modern form, from the USA, of 'Mary' (*see Mary*).

Marina The Latin form of the Greek name 'Pelagia', although sometimes believed to be the feminine of 'Marinus' (there are eleven saints of this name), which is the Latin for 'of the sea'. Little is known of the two early Christian saints of this name.

S.D. 18th July

Marion Originally a diminutive of 'Mary'. It was used throughout the Middle Ages and later, probably in the eighteenth century, led to the spelling 'Marian' (*see Mary*).

Marisa (Marissa) A modern variant of 'Maria' (*see Mary*).

Marjorie The modern form of 'Margery', which was the usual form used throughout the Middle Ages of 'Margaret' (*see Margaret*).

Marlene German in origin it is a contraction of 'Maria Magdalena' (Mary Magdalen), the full and proper name of Marlene Dietrich (1901–92) the German film actress (*see Madeleine*).

Marsha A variant spelling, from the USA of 'Marcia' (*see Marcia*).

Martha From the Aramaic meaning 'lady' or 'mistress', it was the name of one of Christ's disciples, the sister of Lazarus and Mary (John 11:1; Luke 10:38).

Mary The English form of the Hebrew name 'Miriam' meaning 'desired' or 'longed for'. The most popular and enduring of female names throughout Europe ('Marie' French; 'Maria' German; 'Marya' Russian; etc.). It was a popular name at the time of Christ; there was Mary of Magdala, Mary, the mother of James, etc. Its popularity in later centuries was due to the Virgin Mary, the mother of Jesus. It was a common Christian name at first, witness several early Christian saints; then for several hundred years the name of the Mother of God was considered too holy to be used. It was not until the twelfth century that it gradually came to be used throughout Europe and grew in popularity. (There are over 2,000 churches dedicated to 'St Mary the Virgin' throughout England alone.) Many other female names are derived from 'Mary' (*see names commencing Mari-*).

S.D. 15th August

Matilda   The Latin form, used in England from Norman times, of the German name 'Mahtihildis' meaning 'brave little maid'. The medieval vernacular form, used alongside 'Matilda' was 'Maud'; both were common up to the fifteenth century. Both enjoyed a revival in the eighteenth century. There was one saint who was wife of the German King, Henry the Fowler. As a widow she founded four famous German Benedictine monasteries (d. 968).

S.D. 14th March

Maud (Maude)   The English form of the German name 'Mahtihildis' and an alternative form to 'Matilda'. Borne by the wife of William the Conqueror, it was a popular Norman name. The Empress Maud (1102–67) conducted a civil war in England in a quest for the throne; and Tennyson (1855) wrote a poem entitled *Maud*.

Maura   Of Celtic origin, its meaning is uncertain. There are six saints who bore the name, but little is known about any of them.

S.D. 15th January

Maureen   The English form of the Irish name 'Mairin' which is derived from 'Maire', the Irish form of 'Mary' (*see Mary*).

May   A modern name, from the late nineteenth century, being a pet name derived from 'Margaret' or 'Mary'. By the 1920s it had become an independent name.

Meg   Short form of 'Margaret' (*see Margaret*).

Megan (Meagan)   The Welsh short form of 'Margaret' (*see Margaret*).

Melanie   From the Greek '*melaina*' meaning 'dark' or 'black'. The English form comes from the Old French form of the Latin 'Melania'. There are two saints of this name, Melania the Elder (*c.* 342–410) and her granddaughter, Melania the Younger (*c.* 383–438). It was probably introduced into England by the Protestant Hugenots; the name died out for over a century and was reintroduced in the middle of the twentieth century.

S.D. 8th June

Mercedes A Spanish name derived from the title of the Virgin Mary 'Maria de las Mercedes' (Mary of Mercies). When, in Spain, 'Mary' was considered too sacred a name (*see Mary*) to be used, but there was a devotion to the Virgin Mary, her titles were used. It is more frequently found in the USA and France than in Britain.

Mercia   A Latin form of 'Mercy' (*see Mercy*).

Mercy   The seventeenth-century Puritans introduced this name, along with 'Faith', 'Hope' and 'Charity'. It comes from '*merces*', the Latin for 'reward'.

Michaela   The feminine form of 'Michael' (*see Michael*).

Michelle   From the French feminine form of 'Michel' (Michael) (*see Michael*).

Mildred   From the Old English 'Mildthryth' meaning 'gentle counsellor'. This is the name of a seventh-century (d.*c.* 700) Abbess of Minister, Isle of Thanet. Her mother and two sisters were also honoured, by popular acclaim, as saints. The name dropped out of use, but was revived in the nineteenth century.

S.D. 13th July

Miriam   From the Hebrew (although it may originally have been Egyptian) meaning 'desired' or 'longed for'; the English form is 'Mary'. This was the name of the elder sister of Moses (Exod. 2:4–8; 15:20–1 where her son is recorded). It is still a favoured name in the Jewish community (*see Mary*).

Moira (Moyra)   The English form of the Irish name 'Maire', which is the Irish version of 'Mary' (*see Mary*).

Molly   The familiar form of 'Mary' (*see Mary*).

Monica   Probably of African or Phoenician origin as the saint from whom we get this name was born at Carthage in 332. In the Middle Ages it was thought to have come from the Latin '*monere*' meaning 'to advise' or 'to warn', but this is unlikely. By her prayers and example St Monica converted her son, the great St Augustine, Doctor of the Church, to Christianity.

S.D. 27th August

N

Nancy   Its origins are uncertain but it first emerged as a familiar form of 'Ann'; then in the USA became an independent name (*see Ann*).

Naomi   From the Hebrew meaning 'the pleasant one'. It was the name of Ruth's mother-in-law and her story can be found in the Book of Ruth. It was first used as a Christian name in the seventeenth century.

Natalie (Nathalie)   From the Latin '*natalis*' meaning 'birthday', referring to '*Natalis Domini*' (the Birthday of the Lord – Christmas). Under its Latin form 'Natalia' there are three saints who bore the name. It has long been used in France and Germany, and in the twentieth century in Britain.

S.D. 1st December

Nell   The short form of 'Eleanor', e.g. Nell Gwyn's name was Eleanor Gwyn (*see Eleanor*).

Nicola   The Italian feminine form (from the Latin) of 'Nicholas' (*see Nicholas*).

Nicole   The French feminine form of 'Nicholas' (*see Nicholas*).

Nina   The shortened Russian form of 'Ann' (*see Ann*).

Ninette   A name which illustrates how international names have become. It is the French diminutive form of the Russian shortened form of 'Ann'. It came into the English-speaking world in the twentieth century, via France.

O

Odette   The French diminutive of 'Odille' which is the French form of the German name 'Otilla' meaning 'prosperous one'. There was a rather obscure saint of this name, who died *c.* 720.

S.D. *13th December*

Olga   A Russian name of Scandinavian origin derived from the Norse word '*helga*' meaning 'holy'. St Olga, wife of Igor, Duke of Kiev (879–969), was believed to be the first Russian convert to Christianity.

S.D. *11th July*

Olivia (Olive)   Believed to come from the Latin '*oliva*' meaning 'olive'. There are two obscure saints of this name; apart from being virgin-martyrs of the first two centuries, little else is known about either of them. It can be considered as the feminine form of 'Oliver'.

S.D. *5th March*

P

Patience   As with the other names taken from virtues or qualities, like 'Faith', 'Mercy' etc. it was introduced by the Puritans of the seventeenth century. It comes from the Latin word '*patientia*' meaning 'endurance', and probably derived from the verb '*patior*' meaning 'to suffer'. It is one of the seven Christian virtues.

Patricia The feminine form of the Latin 'Patricius' (Patrick). There is an actual St Patricia (d.*c.* 665), a virgin from Constantinople who became a nun at Rome, and is one of the patron saints of Naples.

S.D. (St Patrick) 17th March S.D. (St Patricia) 25th August

Paula The feminine form, from the Latin, of 'Paul' (*see Paul*). There are seven saints of this name; five of whom were martyrs of the early years of Christianity. One was a fourteenth-century nun and the last founded a Religious Teaching Order in the nineteenth century.

S.D. 11th June

Paulette A modern name, originating in France and derived from 'Paula' (*see Paula*).

Pauline The French form of the Latin 'Paulina', which is the feminine of 'Paulinus'. There are twelve saints who bore the name 'Paulinus', most importantly St Paulinus of York (d. 644). However, in the English-speaking world it is commonly accepted as the female equivalent of 'Paul'.

S.D. (St Paulinus of York) 10th October S.D. (St Paul) 29th June

Petra From the Greek '*petra*' meaning 'stone', this is the feminine form of 'Peter' (*see Peter*).

Petrina Another feminine form of 'Peter' (*see Petra and Peter*).

Philippa   The Latin feminine form of 'Philip' (see Philip). Until modern times women were actually called 'Philip' although this Latin form existed and was used in early Christian times. There are four saintly women called 'Philippa'; the first saint was crucified, with a group of martyrs at Perga, Pamphilia, in 220.

S.D. 20th September

Philomena   Thought to be from the Greek verb '*philoumai*', meaning 'I am loved'. There was one St Philomena (d.c. 500) venerated at Ancona, Italy, but nothing is known about her. In 1802 research appeared to have found a second; interest spread, and the name became popular; then further research revealed an error and devotion to her was prohibited in 1961.

S.D. 5th July

Phoebe   From the Greek meaning 'the bright one'. St Paul, in his Letter to the Romans, commends Phoebe, a deaconess, at Cenchreae, near Corinth, to his readers (Rom. 16:1–3). The name was introduced into England after the Reformation.

S.D. 3rd September

Pippa   A familiar form of 'Phillippa' (see Phillippa).

Priscilla   From the Latin name meaning 'of ancient lineage'. In the Acts of the Apostles Luke refers (18:2) to a Priscilla who was the wife of Aquilla. The name was popular among the seventeenth-century Puritans, who first introduced it to the English-speaking world.

S.D. 8th July

Prudence   From the Latin word '*prudentia*' meaning 'prudence'; also the feminine form of 'Prudentius'. There are two little-known male saints of this name and a female,

Blessed Prudentia, a fifteenth-century Italian abbess. The name was popular with the Puritans who associated it with the virtue of prudence.

S.D. 6th May

R

Rachel (Rachael)   From the Hebrew meaning 'ewe'. It was the name of the wife of Jacob (see Gen. 29:9ff) and mother of Joseph and Benjamin (30:25). Always a popular Jewish name it was not used as a Christian name until the seventeenth century.

Raquel   The Spanish form of 'Rachel' (*see Rachel*).

Ramona   The feminine form of 'Raymond' (*see Raymond*).

Rebecca   From the Latin form of the Hebrew name 'Rebekah', which is probably of Aramaic origin; its meaning is not known. It was the name of Isaac's wife (Gen. 24:45ff) and mother of Jacob. Always popular in the Jewish community, it became a common Christian name after the Reformation.

Regina   From the Latin word '*regina*' meaning 'queen'. There was a St Regina (d. 286) a virgin-martyr of Autun, but the name's use comes from the popular title of the Virgin Mary, 'Regina Coeli' (Queen of Heaven) that all medieval Christians would have heard and used.

Reine   The French form of 'Regina' (*see Regina*).

Renée   A French name which comes from the Latin '*renatus*' meaning 'born again'. For the Christians of the Early Church this was a significant baptismal name, for by

Baptism the Christian is 'born again'. (See the words of Jesus, John 3:7.) There were two saints called 'Renatus', the better known being St Renatus (René) Goupil (d. 1642) tortured to death by Iroquois Indians.

S.D. 19th October

Rhoda   From the Greek for 'rose'. It was the name of a very minor New Testament character (see Acts 12:13). It was first used in the English-speaking world by the seventeenth-century Puritans.

Richelle   A modern feminine form of 'Richard', from the French (*see Richard*).

Rita   Before it became an independent name this was the short form of the Spanish 'Margarita' (Margaret) (*see Margaret*).

Roberta   A Latin form of 'Robert' used as the feminine version (*see Robert*).

Rosalie   From the Latin '*rosalia*' referring to a garland of roses. There was a St Rosalia (d. 1160), a Sicilian recluse who became patron saint of Palermo, Sicily.

S.D. 15th July

Rose   The Latin is '*rosa*' (rose) but it seems not to have originated from the Latin but from the German. The common medieval form of the name was 'Rohesia' or 'Roese'. There are two saints of this name; the better known being St Rose of Lima (1586–1617), the first American-born to be canonised as a saint, she is the patron of South America.

S.D. 23rd August

Rosemary   A name which first appeared in the eighteenth century, probably taken from the herb. However, some see it as the combination of the names 'Rose' and 'Mary' (*see Rose and Mary*).

Rosie   A familiar form of 'Rose' or 'Rosemary' (*see Rose and Rosemary*).

Ruth   The name of the biblical character whose story is told in the Book of Ruth. She was a Moabite and the meaning of her name is unknown. It was first used as a Christian name in the seventeenth century and was very popular among the Puritans.

S

Sabina   The feminine form of the Latin name 'Sabinus'. The Sabines were a tribal people conquered by the early Romans (the Sabine Women, subject of classical art). There were ten saints of the early Christian centuries named 'Sabinus', and two who bore the name 'St Sabina'.

S.D. 29th August

Sadie   A familiar form of 'Sarah' (*see Sarah*).

Sally   Originally this was a familiar form of 'Sarah'; however, in the twentieth century it has become an independent name. (*See Sarah*.)

Sara (Sarah)   From the Hebrew meaning 'princess'. The name first appears in the Book of Genesis (11:29), where it is the name of Abram's (later Abraham) wife. At first it is spelt 'Sarai' meaning 'contentious'; later (17:15) God ordered her to be called 'Sarah'. The name was not used in England until the twelfth century, when it was spelt 'Sarra'. The modern spelling appeared in the seventeenth century.

Seraphina   The Latin feminine form of the Hebrew word '*seraphim*' meaning 'noble' or 'ardent believer'. It is, according to Isaiah 6:2, one of the orders of angels. There are two saints of this name in the Christian calendar, neither of them well known.

S.D. 12th March

Serena   The feminine form of the Latin '*serenus*' meaning 'calm' or 'serene'. According to early, and unreliable records, St Serena (d.*c.* 290) was 'sometime wife of the Emperor Diocletian'. Little else is known about her.

S.D. 16th August

Sharon   This has been used as both a male and a female name and first appeared among the seventeenth-century Puritans, who searched the Bible for new Christian names. They found the place name 'I am the rose of Sharon' (coastal plain, Northern Israel) in the Song of Songs (2:1) and used it.

Sharona   Latin style form of 'Sharon' (*see Sharon*).

Sidony   From the Latin feminine form of the name 'Sidonius' meaning 'a man from Sidon' (a Phoenician city). Two saints bore this name, the most important being St Sidonius Apollinaris (*c.* 423–80) who as Bishop of Clermont saved his people from the Goths. The name is also associated with the Greek '*sindon*' meaning 'winding sheet', referring to the burial cloth of Christ, the Shroud of Turin.

S.D. 21st August

Silvia   The original spelling of 'Sylvia' from the Latin for 'wood'. 'Rhea Silvia' was the name of the mother of the twins, Romulus and Remus, who founded the city of Rome. It was also the name of the saintly mother of the Pope (d. 572), St Gregory the Great, who sent St Augustine to convert England.

S.D. 3rd November

Sophia   From the Greek for 'wisdom'. Two third-century martyrs bore the name; a third was the legendary mother of three virgin-martyrs, 'Faith', 'Hope' and 'Charity' who died at Rome. It was later discovered that the account was an allegory to teach how the virtues spring from '*Hagia Sophia*' (holy wisdom).

S.D. 30th September

Sophie   The French form of 'Sophia' (*see Sophia*).

Stella   From the Latin word for 'star'. First used in the sixteenth century, it has since been used in the Roman Catholic community as derived from the title 'Stella Maris' (Star of the Sea), an ancient title given to the Virgin Mary.

Stephanie   From the Latin 'Stephania', used by the early Christians as the feminine form of 'Stephen' (*see Stephen*).

Sue   The short form of 'Susan' or 'Susanna' (*see Susanna*).

Susanna (Susannah)   From the Hebrew meaning 'lily'. There were four shadowy saints who bore this name, but it was the story of the Jewish heroine, in the apocryphal Book of Susannah, and the Elders which caught the imagination of medieval Christians.

S.D. 18th January

Sylvia   Alternative spelling of 'Silvia' (*see Silvia*).

T

Tabitha   This is the Aramaic equivalent of 'Dorcas' meaning 'gazelle' or 'graceful'. It was the name of the woman that was restored to life by St Paul (Acts 9:36–41) (*see Dorcas*).

Talitha   From the Aramaic meaning 'little girl'. As a Christian name it is derived from the words of Jesus (Mark 5:41) 'little girl, arise'.

Tamara   A Russian name derived from the Hebrew 'Tamar' meaning 'date palm'. There are three biblical women who bore this name: the wife of Er, son of Judah (Gen. 38:6); a beautiful sister of Absalom (1 Chron. 3:9); a daughter of Absalom (2 Sam. 14:27).

Tamsin   A shortened form of 'Thomasina' which in medieval times was popular as the feminine form of 'Thomas' (*see Thomas*).

Teresa (Theresa)   A common, and popular, name found in all European countries but its origin and meaning are obscure. It is first found in the fifth century in the form 'Therasia', belonging to the wife of St Paulinus, Bishop of Nola. Its use spread through the fame of St Teresa of Avila (a), the great Spanish mystic (1515–82). There have been four other saints including the French modern popular saint, Thérèse of Lisieux (b) (1873–97).

(a) S.D. 15th October (b) S.D. 1st October

131

Terri   A modern shortened form of 'Teresa' or a feminine form of 'Terry' (*see Teresa*).

Tessa   A familiar form of 'Teresa' (*see Teresa*).

Thea   Shortened form of 'Dorothea' (*see Dorothea*).

Thecla   Derived from the Greek name 'Theokleia' meaning 'divine follower'. It was the name of a first-century saint (there are six other little-known saints) who, according to a very unreliable source, was a follower of St Paul and the first woman Christian martyr.

S.D. 23rd September

Theodora   From the Greek meaning 'gift of God'. (Another version of 'Dorothy'.) It is also the feminine form of 'Theodore'. There are seven saints of this name, the best known being the Empress, wife of Theophilus (d. 867), who struggled to restore the veneration of icons in the Eastern Church.

S.D. 1st April

U

Ursula   From the Latin '*ursa*' meaning 'she-bear'. The story of the fourth-century St Ursula and her virgin companions who died for the Christian faith at Cologne was one of the most popular of the Middle Ages; and the use of the name was widespread.

S.D. 21st October

V

Valerie The French form of the Latin 'Valeria', the feminine form of 'Valerius', probably derived from *valere* meaning 'healthy and strong'. There are three very obscure early Christian martyrs of this name in the Christian calendar.

S.D. 28th April

Vera From the Russian word *vjera* meaning 'faith'. It is the same as the Latin feminine form of *verus* meaning 'true'. The name has only been used this century in the English-speaking world.

Verity From the Latin word *veritas* meaning 'truth'. It was a popular name among the Puritans of the seventeenth century.

Veronica Derived from combining two Latin words *verus* ('true') and *iconicus* ('image'). The name was given to a cloth which was believed to carry the image of Christ's face. According to legend, a woman in the crowd (later called 'Veronica') wiped the face of Jesus as he carried his cross to Calvary. The Eastern Church identifies the woman healed in Matthew 9:20–2.

Victoria The feminine form of 'Victor' from the Latin *victorius* meaning 'victory'. It was hardly known in England before 1837 and the accession of Queen Victoria; however, there are two martyrs of early Christian times of this name.

S.D. 23rd December

Vivian (Vivien)   A name which has been used by both sexes (*see Vivian*).

W

Winifred (Winefred)   The English form of the Welsh name 'Gwenfrewi' meaning 'peaceful friend'. The seventh-century Welsh saint of this name was a historical person but her life has been so decorated with legends that little is known for sure. She was a martyr and associated with the Holy Well, to which for many centuries pilgrimages have been made and cures claimed.

S.D. 3rd November

Y

Yolanda (Yolande)   Of very uncertain origin and meaning. There was a saintly Hungarian woman (d. 1298) of this name, who was the daughter of King Bela IV of Hungary and a niece of St Elizabeth.

S.D. 15th June

Z

Zillah   From the Hebrew meaning 'shade'. It is found in the Book of Genesis where it is the name of one of Lamech's wives (Gen. 4:19). It was introduced into use in Britain by the seventeenth-century Puritans, in their search for new Christian names.

Zita   The origins of this name are obscure; it is believed to come from medieval Tuscany because the saint (1218–72) from whom we get the name was from that part of Italy. She lived and died as a domestic servant and is the patron saint of domestic servants.

S.D. 27th April

Zoe From the Greek meaning 'life'. In the Septuagint (Greek) translation of the Hebrew Bible, the name 'Eve' was translated as 'Zoe'. It was a common Christian name in Byzantine times and there are two little-known saints from that period. It was not used in England until the nineteenth century.

S.D. 5th July